THE AYRSHIRE AND ARRAN COASTAL PATHS

About the author

Keith Fergus is a passionate walker, writer and photographer. His writing on the outdoors, Scottish history and the Scottish language – combined with his striking imagery – has been published in a variety of national magazines, newspapers, calendars and brochures. He also has three photographic books to his name.

Keith has walked all over Scotland, with the mountains and coast particular favourites. Growing up in Glasgow the Ayrshire coast was the most natural (and nearest) place to visit and the best place to enjoy his passions of walking and photography; it still ranks high among his favourite destinations. Over 30 years of visiting and exploring means he has an intimate knowledge of the region, its incredible history, diverse wildlife and breathtaking scenery.

Passionate about the outdoors and the crucial role it plays – particularly in modern life – Keith is never happier than when wandering along a mountain ridge or across a secluded beach. He also runs his own photographic business and photo library, which, under the banner of *Scottish Horizons* www.scottishhorizons.co.uk, produces a range of postcards, greetings cards and calendars. He lives with his wife and two children on the outskirts of Glasgow and is a member of the Outdoor Writers and Photographers Guild.

THE AYRSHIRE AND ARRAN COASTAL PATHS

by Keith Fergus

2 POLICE SQUARE, MILNTHORPE, CUMBRIA LA7 7PY
www.cicerone.co.uk

© Keith Fergus 2011
First Edition 2011
ISBN 978 1 85284 632 9

Printed in China on behalf of Latitude Press Ltd.

A catalogue record for this book is available from the British Library.

All photographs are by the author.

This product includes mapping data licensed from Ordnance Survey® with the permission of the Controller of Her Majesty's Stationery Office. © Crown copyright 2011. All rights reserved. Licence number PU100012932.

Advice to Readers

Readers are advised that, while every effort is made by our authors to ensure the accuracy of guidebooks as they go to print, changes can occur during the lifetime of an edition. Please check Updates on this book's page on the Cicerone website (www.cicerone.co.uk) before planning your trip. We would also advise that you check information about such things as transport, accommodation and shops locally. Even rights of way can be altered over time. We are always grateful for information about any discrepancies between a guidebook and the facts on the ground, sent by email to info@cicerone.co.uk or by post to Cicerone, 2 Police Square, Milnthorpe LA7 7PY, United Kingdom.

Front cover: Looking across the Firth of Clyde to Arran from the summit of The Knock (Day 11)

CONTENTS

INTRODUCTION 9
A short history of Ayrshire. 10
A short history of Arran. 13
Arran's geology. 14
Wildlife 15
Getting there 16
Getting around 17
When to go 18
Accommodation. 18
Food and drink. 19
Money 19
Keeping in touch 20
What to take. 20
The Scottish Outdoor Access Code 21
Waymarks and access. 21
Maps 22
Emergency services 22
Using this guide 22
Timing 23

AYRSHIRE   Day 1 Glenapp to Ballantrae 25
                Day 2 Ballantrae to Girvan 35
                Day 3 Girvan to Dunure 46
                Day 4 Dunure to Troon 61
                Day 5 Troon to Ardrossan 78

ARRAN   Day 6 Brodick to Lochranza 94
                Day 7 Lochranza to Blackwaterfoot. 107
                Day 8 Blackwaterfoot to Kildonan. 118
                Day 9 Kildonan to Brodick 130

AYRSHIRE   Day 10 Ardrossan to Largs. 145
                Day 11 Largs to Skelmorlie 157

APPENDIX A Route summary table 167
APPENDIX B Accommodation. 168
APPENDIX C Public transport options 172
APPENDIX D Useful information 173

Goat Fell rises majestically above Brodick Bay (Day 6)

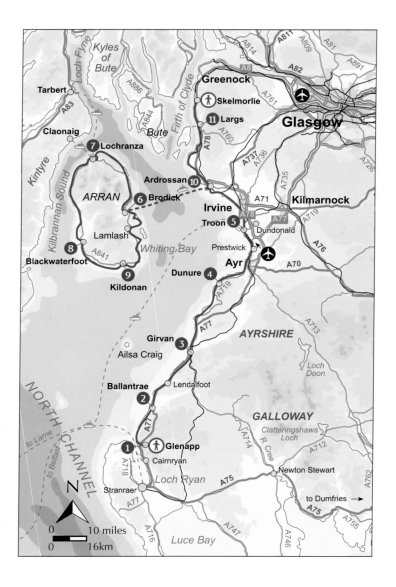

The beautiful clear waters below Turnberry Lighthouse (Day 3)

INTRODUCTION

A wonderful sandy beach leads towards Bennan Head (Day 8)

Ayrshire, is that where the poet Rabbie Burns was born?

If the question asked was 'what do you know about Ayrshire?' this may well be the answer. But there is more, so much more. The fantastic Ayrshire Coastal Path strikes its course for 94 miles from Glenapp in the south to Skelmorlie in the north. Add to this the Arran Coastal Path, which circumnavigates its way round that magical island for 60 miles, and what you have is a truly magnificent coastal walk.

But coastal walking is just along beaches is it not?

Well, yes and no. Yes, the Ayrshire and Arran Coastal Paths travel over beaches (and beautiful beaches at that) but this route also journeys across a magnificent and diverse landscape that is home to some remarkable scenery, while a substantial portion of the route takes you away from the well-beaten track and enables walkers to observe the rugged beauty of the coastline and enjoy its peace and quiet. Furthermore, the coastline has a wealth of wonderful architecture: from the instantly recognisable castles Culzean and Brodick to smaller, hidden gems such as the Kennedy Mausoleum and Glenapp Church. Add to the mix a series of sublime beaches, secluded coves, fantastic wildlife, erratic rocks and boulders, a historical legacy of huge importance, world famous golf courses, old paths

9

and roads and, yes, Scotland's most important literary figure Robert Burns, and you have an enormously rewarding long-distance walk.

The route can be walked in 11 days by an average walker but, despite it being well waymarked, a substantial portion crosses some surprisingly remote ground, open moorland and rocky terrain, so reasonable map and navigational skills are a prerequisite. The route is well served by an excellent public transport infrastructure and therefore it can also be broken down into lovely one or two-day sections.

The Ayrshire & Arran Coastal Paths begin in the tiny hamlet of Glenapp and cross wild, open moorland to reach the village of Ballantrae. Travelling north, the route passes through the bustling towns of Girvan, Ayr and Troon to reach Ardrossan, where the ferry crosses the Firth of Clyde to Brodick. Four wonderful days are then spent circumnavigating the coast of Arran, taking in Brodick, Lochranza, Blackwaterfoot and Kildonan. Back on the mainland, the route's beautiful coastal scenery continues on its way to Largs and its culmination at Skelmorlie. This is Scotland's celebrated wild and windswept west coast at its finest.

A SHORT HISTORY OF AYRSHIRE

Like much of the British Isles, evidence shows that there has been human activity in the area for many thousands of years but it was not until

the early part of the 12th century that the historic shire of Ayr, with borders stretching from Inverclyde in the north to Galloway in the south, was established. The ancient districts of Kyle, Carrick and Cunninghame were amalgamated at this time to form the shire and Ayr became (as it still is today) the area's main town. Prior to this Carrick belonged to Galloway while Kyle and Cunninghame were, surprisingly, part of Northumbria. Going back even further to the second century, southern Scotland was home to the people known as the Damnonii. Very little is known about the tribe but they settled in the likes of Ayrshire, Renfrewshire, Lanarkshire and as far north as Stirlingshire, possibly occupying the landscape in and around the fort of Dumyat.

Largs, at the northern end of the Ayrshire coastline, played a momentous role in Scotland's development when the Battle of Largs was fought on the outskirts of the town on the 2nd of October 1263. The battle was crucial in bringing to an end the Scottish-Norwegian War and settling disputed lands along much of Scotland's western seaboard, which had been in Norwegian possession since the 12th century.

Ayrshire also lays claim to being the birthplace of both Robert the Bruce (in 1274 at Turnberry) and William Wallace (in around 1272 at Ellerslie), although both Dumfriesshire and Renfrewshire (the Bruce and Wallace respectively) have always contested

Beautiful dusk reflections at Largs Marina (Day 10)

this. What is definite is that much of the early lives of these two national icons were played out in Ayrshire. The Bruce held the first meeting of the Scottish Parliament at the Church of St John in Ayr, the year after his famous 1314 victory over Edward II's English army at Bannockburn. Wallace torched an English garrison at Ayr in 1297 in what has since become known as the 'Burning of the Barns of Ayr'.

During the early 13th century much of the land along the mainland Ayrshire coastline was owned by the Kennedy Clan, which had separate factions including the Bargany and the Cassillis Kennedys. The history of the clan is a hostile one, with much blood shed over the centuries. Other major landowners within Ayrshire included The Wallaces of Craigie and the Montgomerys of Eglinton. The first

traceable Kennedy ancestor is John Kennedy of Dunure, who was granted the lands of Carrick in 1358 by King David II and, as land equalled power, John Kennedy became one of the most influential men in the southwest. In 1360 he made the crucial acquisition of Cassillis House near Maybole, which would eventually become the seat of the Kennedys. In around 1457, the head of the family at the time, Gilbert, took the title 1st Lord Kennedy and this title was thereafter handed down to future generations. Later, in 1509, the title Earl of Cassillis was created for the clan and the first to bear it was David. Succeeding him as the 2nd Earl of Cassillis was his son Gilbert (simultaneously he became the 4th Lord Kennedy), who seemed to set the tone for the family's successive generations by being involved in

11

Almost six miles of uninterrupted sand lie between Barassie and Irvine (Day 5)

several unlawful deeds, which would then typically necessitate acts of retribution, usually by the Bargany faction of the Kennedy clan.

The 15th and 16th centuries saw Ayrshire under control of the shire's churches and abbeys, but with the religious upheaval of the Protestant Reformation in 1560 the ownership of land instead came under the control of local landowners. Roman Catholic attempts to regain control of Scotland after 1560 gave rise to the Covenanters, whose supporters fought to uphold the Reformation. The turbulence of the time led to much infighting and many deaths in Ayrshire.

Agriculture, mining, fishing, steel-making, shipbuilding and manufacturing textiles such as cotton and cloth have all played an important part in the development of Ayrshire

in recent times, although with the decline of heavy industry within the region (and more recently the closing of the Johnnie Walker whisky plant in Kilmarnock) it has relied somewhat on 20th century industries like computing and chemicals.

However, tourism has come to play a major role in Ayrshire's economy and this is mainly due to one particular sport and to one man. The sport is golf. Ayrshire is the only county in Britain to contain three golf courses that have played host to an Open Championship, with Prestwick holding the very first in 1860, followed by many more. Prestwick has now been taken out of the tournament's rotation but many have also been held at Turnberry and at Royal Troon, which both remain choices for the organisers. The one man who has created a cottage industry in his own right is Robert Burns. Born on the 25th of January 1759 in Alloway near Ayr, Burns' poems are renowned world-wide. He has become a cultural icon for Scots, both in Scotland and in the many expat communities around the world.

A SHORT HISTORY OF ARRAN

Lying some 15 miles off the Ayrshire mainland, Arran translates (depending on the source) either from the Gaelic *Ar Rinn* as 'place of the peaked hills' or from the Irish *Arainn*, meaning kidney-shaped. Certainly, both make sense. Gaelic plays a large part in the names of Arran's spectacular mountains (Cir Mhòr and Caisteal Abhail, for instance) while Old Norse has left its mark on Glen Rosa, Glen Sannox and the island's highest peak, Goat Fell, which climbs to 2866ft (874m) above Brodick Bay; itself a translation from the Old Norse *Breithr Vik*, which means Broad Bay. This association with the Old Norse language stretches back to around the 9th or 10th centuries, when Arran was under the ownership (as were many of Scotland's present islands) of the Norwegian crown. It was not until after the Battle of Largs in the 13th century that it fell into Scottish hands. In fact it was at Lamlash Bay on Arran's eastern side that Norway's king, Hakon IV, reassembled his defeated army after the battle.

Again, like the Ayrshire mainland, people have left their mark on Arran for more than 5000 years. The wonderfully bleak Machrie Moor, with its amazing stone circles, is just one spot on the island that contains evidence of human activity from that time. Neolithic, Bronze Age and Iron Age sites have all been excavated.

After Viking rule ended things became very complicated, especially when Scotland's King Alexander III died in 1286, leaving no immediate heir (the nearest descendant was his four-year old granddaughter Margaret, the 'Maid of Norway', so named for being the child of King Eric II of Norway and Alexander III's daughter, Margaret). Things were complicated even further by the Maid of Norway's death in the Orkney Islands in 1290, which occurred during her crossing of the North Sea to be crowned Queen of Scotland. Over the next 20 years or so Scotland's claimants to the vacant throne were plunged into a variety of feuds. One such rivalry eventually led to the 1306 murder of John Comyn (known as 'The Red' Comyn) in Dumfries by his then competitor for the crown Robert the Bruce. This was an infamous event in Scottish history, having occurred at the altar of the town's Greyfriars church.

In the same year, the Bruce was crowned King of Scots. After defeat in battle against occupying English forces he fled Scotland for a time, ending up on Rathlin Island off the Northern Ireland coast, before ultimately finding his way to Arran and taking shelter at King's Cave, a short distance north of Blackwaterfoot. It is claimed that this was the setting for his famous encounter with the determined spider, which refused to give up building its web on a slippy cave wall until it succeeded. This gave the Bruce the inspiration he needed to return to the mainland and continue the fight for Scottish independence.

Over the subsequent centuries, and certainly in some part due to its position in the Firth of Clyde, Arran became continually caught up in various dynastic struggles (particularly between the clans of the Stewarts and the Hamiltons). Its population decreased in 1828 during the Clearances instigated by Alexander Douglas-Hamilton, the 10th Duke of Hamilton, and it was hit hard by the Potato Famine of 1845. The number has varied over the years, but the current population of the island is around 5000.

By the end of the 19th century Arran had finally begun to establish proper links with the mainland, with piers having been built at Brodick, Lamlash, Whiting Bay and Lochranza. Since then agriculture and tourism have become the backbone of Arran's economy. When the Caledonian MacBrayne ferry began making regular, daily sailings to the island in the 1970s, Arran became one of Scotland's most popular tourist destinations.

ARRAN'S GEOLOGY

The wonderful natural arena of Arran was formed around 400 million years ago and its layers of rock, including Dalradian and Ordovician schists as well as red sandstone, have made the island a playground for geologists for decades. James Hutton, the 'father of modern geology', visited Arran in the

Looking along Arran's peaceful western coast from The Postman's Path (Day 7)

late 1800s and found evidence that transformed his ideas concerning the earth's age and formation. The island is split by the Highland Boundary Fault Line, a geological fault that traverses Scotland from west coast to east and which separates the country into its two distinctly different regions, the Highlands and the Lowlands. Arran's northern half is dominated by igneous rocks formed around 50-60 million years ago while the southern end is formed by Devonian and Carboniferous rocks estimated to be around 380 million years old. Yet it wasn't until the beginnings of deglaciation at the end of the last Ice Age, approximately 10,000 years ago, that the magnificent mountains of Arran started to emerge from under the ice and the island's wonderful glens began to gouge their way through its landscape.

There are many wonderfully erratic glacial boulders clearly visible right round Arran's coastline and the huge, shapely boulders at Corrie are particularly beautiful.

WILDLIFE

The Ayrshire and Arran Coastal Paths are teeming with wildlife and feature a particularly diverse birdlife. This ranges from common coastal species like the black-headed gull, herring gull, oystercatcher, razorbill and guillemot to seasonal birds such as the common tern, grebe, golden plover and goldeneye. The great cliffs near the Heads of Ayr, Ballantrae and round much of Arran are home to birds of prey including buzzards, kestrels and sparrowhawks while the wilder, open landscapes above Glenapp and Largs accommodate moorland birds such as grouse, curlew and meadow pipit.

On quieter sections of the route you may well spot a reclusive roe deer, a contrast to the many sheep and cattle on view. Both common and grey seals are a regular sight off-shore, especially round Arran. The marvellous sight of a sea otter may also be glimpsed round the island's coast. Basking sharks (the world's second biggest fish), dolphins and minke whales have also occasionally been seen, especially from ferries. Arran is one of the few remaining areas of Britain where there is a healthy population of red squirrels, its larger grey cousin never having been introduced to the island.

Holy Isle, sitting just off Arran at Lamlash (a short ferry trip to the island leaves from the harbour at Lamlash), is home to wild goats, Soay sheep and Eriskay ponies. Rabbits, hares, adders, lizards, toads, butterflies, dragonflies and damselflies can also be seen along the Ayrshire and Arran coasts if you keep your eyes peeled.

During spring and summer the sheer variety of wildflowers is fantastic. Bluebells, red campion, wood anemone, field mouse-ear, common scurvy grass, sea campion and sea pinks are just a small selection of the plants that quite literally brighten the paths.

15

The first ferry docks at Brodick after crossing the Firth of Clyde from Ardrossan (Day 6)

For much of the route the conspicuous outline of Ailsa Craig (also known as Paddy's Milestone as it lies approximately halfway between Belfast and Glasgow) is a near-constant sight and there are regular sailings from Girvan for visitors to the island. A day trip is highly recommended. The granite sentinel rises to over 1100ft from the Firth of Clyde and is a Sight of Special Scientific Interest as, with nearly 40,000 breeding pairs, it is home to Britain's third-largest gannet colony. Even from the mainland, or from the southern and eastern shores of Arran, you can see these fantastic seabirds circling the seas round Ailsa Craig. Fulmar, kittiwake, shag, razorbill and (since the eradication of rats on the island in 1991) an increasing number of puffins also breed here. In the 1860s puffins had numbered in the hundreds of thousands before the rat managed to hitch a ride onto the island. Ailsa Craig's position, some 15 miles from the Ayrshire coast in the Firth of Clyde, and the fact that footfall is limited, means over 200 species of plants have been recorded on the island.

GETTING THERE

Air
The Ayrshire coastline has its own airport. Glasgow Prestwick Airport www.gpia.co.uk 0871 223 0700 (UK), 00 44 1292 511000 (International), sits on the outskirts of Prestwick and has excellent connections to other British airports and many European destinations.

Sea
A ferry from Larne docks at Cairnryan, which lies only a few miles from the start of Day 1 at Glenapp. There is also a ferry from Larne that docks at Troon www.poferries.com 0871 66 44 999 (UK), 01 407 34 34 (ROI). For Arran, daily services leave Ardrossan for Brodick and from Claonaig (Kintyre) to Lochranza www.calmac. co.uk 01475 650100.

Rail
Scotrail, www.scotrail.co.uk 0845 601 5929, provide excellent rail links to the Ayrshire coast with a direct link to Largs, Ardrossan, Ayr and many of the Ayrshire coastal towns from Glasgow Central station.

Bus
Scottish Citylink, www.citylink.co.uk 0871 266 33 33, run direct services from Edinburgh or Glasgow to Stranraer, which stop at Glenapp. Stagecoach, www.stagecoachbus.com 01292 613 500, run a direct service from Dumfries to Stranraer and then another from Stranraer to Glenapp.

Road
From Glasgow follow the M8 south to junction 22 and exit onto the M77. Follow this south for approximately 15 miles until the M77 merges with the A77 and then continue south, following signs for Stranraer. The A77 continues through many Ayrshire towns and villages such as Maybole, Kirkoswald, Girvan and Ballantrae to reach Glenapp, which is approximately 11 miles north of Stranraer. If travelling from the south follow the M6 and cross the border to join the M74 at Gretna. Leave the M74 at Junction 22 (Gretna) onto the A75 and follow this for around 90 miles, going through Dumfries and bypassing Castle Douglas and Newton Stewart to reach Stranraer. From there follow the A77 north for 11 miles to reach Glenapp.

GETTING AROUND

Trains
Scotrail provide regular, daily trains from Glasgow Central to Wemyss Bay (a short walk from the north end of Skelmorlie) and to Ayr. No direct rail service links Glenapp with Skelmorlie although all the towns along the Ayrshire coast have their own stations.

Buses on the mainland
There is no direct bus route between Glenapp and Skelmorlie but Stagecoach operates regular, daily services to all the towns along the route.

Buses on Arran
Stagecoach provides an excellent bus service right round Arran. Regular, daily services leave from Brodick Ferry Terminal and stop at all locations en route.

All public transport information should be checked before setting out. See Appendix C for various options.

WHEN TO GO

The routes can be walked at any time of the year, but the months between April and October offer the best conditions to enjoy them. Some sections are long (as far as 18 miles) and, although these can be broken down to suit, they do require ample daylight. During winter the beginning and end of the route may well finish in the dark.

The spring, summer and autumn months also provide the best opportunities to view the wonderful plants and animals en route and allow the walks to proceed in, hopefully, reasonable weather.

It also has to be taken into account that on Arran there is always the chance, particularly during winter, of strong winds. These could lead to ferry cancellations that would leave you island-bound with disrupted plans.

The routes cross a lot of farmland, therefore be aware that during spring the lambing and calving season is in full flow.

ACCOMMODATION

The Ayrshire and Arran Coastal paths are well served with accommodation including various hotels, B&Bs, hostels and campsites. Naturally, however, there are a few areas that prove to be exceptions. There is no accommodation at all in Glenapp and very little after Ballantrae until you reach Girvan, apart from some off-route options that would require you to make other travel arrangements, as well as adding extra time into your schedule. Bearing that in

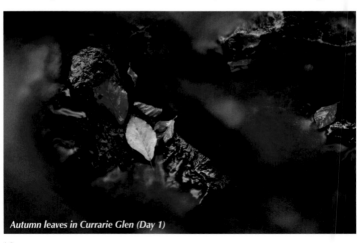

Autumn leaves in Currarie Glen (Day 1)

Legend says Bennane Head was the home of the notorious Scottish cannibal Sawney Bean (Day 2)

mind, this book has been written so that each day finishes where there is somewhere to stay. The further north you go on the mainland the more there is a marked increase in your options. Arran is also very well served for overnight stays although places to stay between Lochranza and Blackwaterfoot are sparse. Accommodation should be booked well in advance, especially in summer. There is a basic accommodation list in Appendix B but for up-to-date details please contact the Ayrshire and Arran Tourist Board www.ayrshire-arran.com 0845 22 55 121.

FOOD AND DRINK

Like the variety of accommodation on offer, the route is predominantly well served for refreshments with many shops, restaurants, cafés and pubs but, similarly, there are some areas where these facilities are thin on the ground. There are no options on Day 1 until you reach Ballantrae, while those between there and Girvan on Day 2 are also limited. The same can be said for Arran, where a lot of the route is well away from the beaten track and it can prove to be several hours before any shop is passed. Consequently, adequate supplies of food and drink should be taken, particularly when options for buying food and drink are limited.

MONEY

While the hotels, restaurants, pubs and shops along the route will take both cash and credit cards, be aware that a few may not and, as the route

Ayr seafront from Deil's Dyke (Day 4)

is predominantly rural, it may be a couple of days until a bank or ATM is available. It is always best to carry enough money to cover at least two days' walking. There are several post offices en route with cash withdrawal facilities, while many of the larger supermarkets offer a cashback service.

KEEPING IN TOUCH

All of the major towns and some of the smaller villages along the route have post offices. Internet access is limited to the larger towns and although mobile phone reception is generally good, there will be times when it is restricted in more remote spots.

WHAT TO TAKE

If you are setting out to complete the Ayrshire and Arran Coastal Paths in one go then a light rucksack with waterproof, maps, compass and a change of clothing for the evening are essential. There are also a few burns and rivers to cross as well as some boggier sections that may result in wet feet, so a change of socks is recommended. A lot of the walking is rough so a good pair of walking shoes or boots is vital, as are good navigational and map reading skills, which may be required depending on the weather.

A note of tide times is important (see the Timing section on page 23), as the height of the tide on several

THE SCOTTISH OUTDOOR ACCESS CODE

Many people make their living along the length of the Ayrshire and Arran Coastal Paths and many more visit the area throughout the year. Furthermore, the route is home to an incredible diversity of wildlife. Please be aware of all this when walking the route and exercise your access rights responsibly. You can do so by following the Scottish Outdoor Access Code, the main points of which are listed below.

To find out more about the code please visit www.outdooraccess-scotland.com.

1. Take responsibility for your own actions.
2. Respect people's privacy and peace of mind. When close to a house or garden, keep a sensible distance, use a path or track if there is one and take extra care not to disturb at night.
3. Help land managers and others to work safely and effectively. Do not hinder land management operations and follow advice from land managers. Respect requests for reasonable limitations on when and where you can go.
4. Care for your environment. Do not disturb wildlife, leave the environment as you find it and follow a path or track if there is one.
5. Keep dogs under proper control. Do not take them through fields of calves or lambs, and dispose of their waste properly.

occasions will determine when to start your day's walking. If the route is to be broken down into one-day sections then all of the above applies. The exceptions are that a lighter day pack would suffice and that it is necessary to take a note of public transport times, as the routes are linear and require buses or trains to return you to your starting point.

WAYMARKS AND ACCESS

Waymarks throughout the route are excellent but when crossing open stretches of moorland keep your eyes peeled for the relevant marker posts. Similarly, routes can take several turns through the streets of busy towns so keep a close lookout for directional changes. The route follows accessible land and has been set up with the full co-operation of landowners, local councils and residents. It passes through farms, near to people's homes and gardens, golf courses and the streets where people live. All this must be taken into account when walking the route and the Scottish Outdoor Access Code must be obeyed.

Margaret, Ballantrae – one of the many charming boats to be found en route (Day 2)

For the mainland:
- Sheet 309 Stranraer and the Rhins
- Sheet 317 Ballantrae, Barr and Barrhill
- Sheet 326 Ayr and Troon
- Sheet 333 Kilmarnock and Irvine
- Sheet 341 Greenock, Largs and Millport

For Arran:
- Sheet 361 Isle of Arran

Route symbols on OS map extracts

~~~ route

~~~ alternative route

(↑) start point

(↑) finish point

◀ direction of walk

For OS symbols key see OS maps.

MAPS

Four Ordnance Survey Landranger maps (1:50,000 scale) cover the Ayrshire & Arran Coastal Paths.

For the mainland:
- Sheet 76 Girvan
- Sheet 70 Ayr, Kilmarnock and Troon
- Sheet 63 Firth of Clyde

For Arran:
- Sheet 69 Isle of Arran

Furthermore, six Ordnance Survey Explorer Maps (1:25,000 scale) cover the route.

EMERGENCY SERVICES

All emergency services (including mountain rescue and coastguard) can be reached by dialling 999 or 112 from a mobile phone. Make sure that mobiles are always charged.

USING THIS GUIDE

The book has primarily been written as a continuous route, although each section can be walked as a day route using the area's excellent public transport. Each day has been written to finish where accommodation, meals and provisions are easily attainable (except Lochranza, **Day 6**, which has hotels but no shop). Further points to remember are as follows:

- Some of the sections can prove quite long and if this is the case then the route can, in most cases, be broken down further into easier chunks.
- A couple of sections do not pass a shop en route, so it is advisable to stock up on the day's provisions before setting out.
- A couple of alternative routes, as well as optional detours, are marked on the relevant maps within the book.

TIMING

Route information boxes list the approximate times that you can expect routes to take. These are based on the abilities of a reasonably fit walker and take into account mileage, the difficulty of the terrain and the level of ascent and descent. Some of the routes cross rough, uneven ground, which can significantly slow your progress, so give yourself enough time to complete each route and consider the weather conditions and how much daylight you can expect at different seasons in the year. Ensure you take into account variables such as rest stops and time taken for photographs. As can be expected of coastal walking, the tide can also play its part in considering how long each route will take to complete.

Weather vanes near the Robert Burns Birthplace Museum depict the poet's greatest works, such as Tam o' Shanter (Day 4)

Ardrossan's North Bay grants another wonderful view of Arran (Day 10)

It is crucial that tide times are thoroughly checked before setting out, as several sections can be impassable or extremely awkward at high tide. This can result in slow progress and could therefore prove disruptive to your plans or could even mean missing the next ferry, bus or train. Go to www.bbc.co.uk/weather/coast/tides for relevant information. Sections where the tide may prove problematic are highlighted in this guide's route text, so check the information on the website before setting out.

One or two days?

Some of the longer routes can easily be broken down into shorter two-day sections. On the mainland **Day 4 Dunure to Troon** and **Day 5 Troon to Ardrossan** could be broken down further by spending the night at Alloway, Ayr, Prestwick, Troon or Irvine. All have accommodation as well as a selection of bars and restaurants to enjoy a night out. Details can be found in Appendix B.

Four days or more?

The four days on Arran could be easily extended to a week, allowing plenty of time to explore the fantastic island. Both Corrie and Sannox have accommodation, which, if you do choose to spend the night, would allow two days to complete **Day 6 Brodick to Lochranza**. Catacol or Pirnmill could be reached from either Corrie or Sannox but there is limited accommodation on Arran's western side. There is then very little in the way of accommodation between Pirnmill and Blackwaterfoot. The only place to stay between Blackwaterfoot and Kildonan is the fantastic Lagg Hotel and a night spent here is great. Options then increase at Kildonan, Whiting Bay and Lamlash, as each offers a variety of accommodation and places to eat, meaning the time spent on Arran can be extended to suit.

DAY 1
Glenapp to Ballantrae

Start	Glenapp NX 074 746
Finish	Kennedy Mausoleum, Ballantrae NX 083 824
Distance	8½ miles (13.5 km)
Time	4 hours
Maps	OS Landranger 76; OS Explorer 317
Terrain	This route is on mostly rugged moorland tracks and paths, which can be indistinct on occasion and sometimes boggy. A couple of sections are also quite steep. The initial climb from Glenapp is through forest before farm roads and a short section of pavement beside the busy A77 lead into Ballantrae.
Refreshments	There is a shop and hotel in Ballantrae.
Public Transport	A regular Stagecoach bus from Ballantrae to Stranraer stops at Glenapp. See Appendix C for details.

The first day of the Ayrshire and Arran Coastal Paths is a short one. Glenapp to Girvan in a single day is feasible but it is long, whereas Glenapp to Ballantrae provides a short but memorable first day and guarantees fresh legs for the longer days ahead. An initial walk through forest climbs onto open moorland above Glenapp. Almost immediately you are struck by the rugged and remote nature of the coast, with much of it well away from any main roads. A good track descends through lovely Currarie Glen and then climbs steeply onto a cliff-top path towards Ballantrae providing magnificent views across Loch Ryan to Galloway and across the Firth of Clyde to Ailsa Craig, Arran, Kintyre and Ireland. Along this section the path becomes indistinct at times but the route is well waymarked when necessary. A singletrack road then passes through some farms (dogs should be kept on leads for the majority of this route) and the day ends at Ballantrae where a stroll around Kennedy Mausoleum is highly recommended. Ballantrae has a shop, a hotel and several B&Bs.

The Ayrshire Coastal Path is a 94-mile route that show-cases some of Scotland's finest scenery, but it has a rela-tively understated start point at the humble surrounds of

Glenapp. Consisting of only a few houses and a very fine church, Glenapp nonetheless provides a peaceful backdrop to the route's start and it is a lovely location to begin a long-distance walk.

Glenapp can be reached by either car or bus and although there is a very small car park across the road from Glenapp Church there is room here for only three or four cars, so it is advisable to use the excellent bus service to drop you at the bottom of the lane leading to the church. If you choose to drive, walk from the car park past Old School House and as the road end is reached turn left to cross the A77. If you take the bus, get off at Glenapp Church and simply walk up the track to the church.

GLENAPP CHURCH

Built in 1850, Glenapp Church was originally a chapel-of-ease for the villagers of nearby Ballantrae. Many towns and villages in Scotland at this time had a chapel-of-ease, which were built to solve the problems of worshippers who could not travel to the larger parish churches; the distance and terrain between Glenapp and Ballantrae would have been too difficult for many during the 19th century. With seating for approximately 70, it is one of the smallest churches in Scotland. In 1985 the church became united with the larger church in Ballantrae. Known locally as The Glen Kirk, it is one of the many fine buildings to be found along the Ayrshire coast.

It is a beautiful little building with lovely stained glass windows, one of which commemorates Elsie MacKay, a British actress and member of the Inchcape family (Glenapp is their family seat) who died while attempting to fly across the Atlantic Ocean in 1928. The graveyard also contains the tombstone of her father James Lyle MacKay, the 1st Earl of Inchcape (a title in the peerage of the United Kingdom that was created in 1929). Its elaborate design includes the carved figures of an eagle, owl, lion and tiger. The memorials to the 2nd Earl, Kenneth MacKay and the 3rd, Kenneth James William MacKay can also be seen in the graveyard. The beauty of the church really sets the scene for the walk ahead.

After exploring the church walk back down the path to reach the A77 and, taking care, cross the busy road to reach the start point of the Ayrshire Coastal Path. A good

track leads to an old bridge over the **Water of App** and then descends to another bridge, the track continuing through lovely mixed woodland. It provides easy walking as you pass **Craiganlea House** on the left, then it bears right at a waymarked sign to climb steadily, passing beneath the slopes of **Sandloch Hill**.

The Ayrshire and Arran Coastal Paths begin near the attractive Glenapp Church

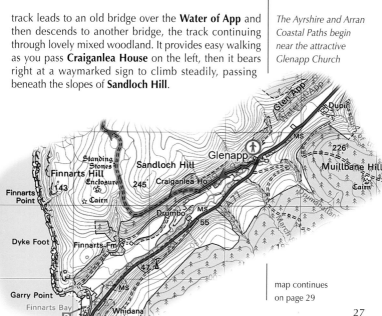

map continues on page 29

27

The superb views continue as you walk north with Arran, Ailsa Craig and Kintyre all visible

Here the views across Loch Ryan towards Galloway are superb.

As the stony track climbs, go through a wooden gate that takes you above the line of trees. ◄ Corsewall Lighthouse is visible at the northern tip of the Rhins of Galloway peninsula (the southern tip of which is the most southerly point in Scotland) as it guides the ferries travelling to and from Northern Ireland into the loch. The track then continues high onto open moorland, where it may surprise you to find such a wild landscape.

Although the path here alternates between grassy and stony the route makes for easy progress. A fence runs to the left of the path with **Finnarts Hill** rising beyond it, while the slopes of Sandloch Hill to the right are vibrant with a thick covering of heather during the summer months. As it continues north the track becomes less steep and passes through a wooden gate at an **old sheep enclosure**, before it reaches another gate.

Go through the gate to continue onto a path that becomes grassier with **Penderry Hill** rising to the right. Windswept moorland is all around but as two standing stones are passed the views west to Kintyre (and Ireland on very clear days) are superb. It is here that the first real views of the rugged Ayrshire coastline can be enjoyed.

As the track descends quite steeply to the north it bears right then flattens out, with gorse bushes to the right and a dry stone dyke to the left, before it passes through another wooden gate.

Two more wooden gates are passed on this track. After going through the second, stick to the main track and ignore the indistinct path descending to the left, which leads to **Portandea**. Go through two more gates to reach a junction of dry stone dykes. From here the level grassy track leads through mixed trees of hawthorn and gorse and there are expansive views that provide the first look at Ailsa Craig, its wonderful profile a mainstay throughout much of the route.

map continues on page 30

The wonderful, distinctive profile of Ailsa Craig rises out of the Firth of Clyde, seen here from Ballantrae

29

AILSA CRAIG

The distinctive cone of Ailsa Craig, which lies some 15 miles off the Ayrshire Coast, rises sharply to over 1100ft in height and has a diameter of approximately one mile. The island is renowned worldwide due to the quality of its granite, used in the production of curling stones, and quarrying took place on the island for many years. Quarrying has now stopped but loose pieces of granite are still taken to be used for curling stones, the production of which still takes place in the Ayrshire village of Mauchline. Ailsa Craig is a popular tourist destination with daily sailings from Girvan allowing visitors to walk on the island and view the wonderful birdlife that calls Ailsa Craig home.

The track then descends slightly to a fork in the road. Go right here (passing a couple of farm buildings on the left) before the track levels out into mixed woodland consisting of beech, birch, hawthorn, and rowan with the surrounding landscape becoming more agricultural. The track makes for easy and enjoyable walking and, as it sweeps 90° round to the left, crosses an old bridge to develop into a farm road.

map continues on page 32

The road continues on to reach a waymarked sign where a track bears left towards the small rise of **Craigangal**. Continue down this track until it turns right. Walk along the flat farm track with Craigangal now to the left and views of Carlock Hill, Milgarva and Green Benan to the right. Just after a bend in the track, go through a wooden gate which in turn gives way to another wooden gate.

The track then descends past an old ruined cottage and at this point becomes boggier and rougher. Walk down the track towards the coast through lovely **Currarie Glen** with the

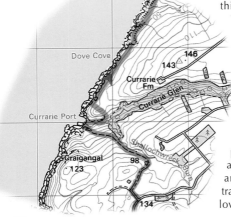

Dove Cove

146
143

Currarie Fm

Currarie Glen

Currarie Port

Craigangal
123

Shallochwreck

98

134

30

Toadstools in Currarie Glen

attractive waters of the **Shallochwreck Burn** tumbling to the right of the track. Kintyre is directly ahead as the track continues to descend steeply to the beautiful cove of **Currarie Port**: a real hidden gem that is unreachable except on foot or by boat. This wild, rocky and wind-swept cove is a great example of the fantastic scenery on offer all along the Ayrshire coastline.

Once Currarie Port is reached, cross the beach to pick up a path that keeps to the right of the burn and then go through a gate. A stony and eroded path then climbs steeply, with a sharp drop to the right affording great views across Currarie Glen. The mixed woodland of the glen looks stunning during the autumn months.

At the top of the slope go through a metal gate then turn left to walk along an indistinct path that climbs steadily between bracken on the left and a fence to the right. A short climb leads to the top of the hill and to a waymarked sign at a gate pointing straight ahead. Go through the gate and walk along the path between a dyke and a fence. ▶ Upon reaching the end of the dyke cross it and bear right onto an open field from which a narrow path can be followed with steep cliffs to the left and a

Take care as the path is very narrow here and the walking underfoot is quite rough.

31

wall continuing to the right. This path leads towards the conspicuous profile of Downan Hill and is one of the finest sections of the entire route, with exemplary views extending across the Firth of Clyde to Arran as well as further along the Ayrshire Coast.

Walk northeast along the path, passing a waymarked post until a fence is reached. Follow the line of the fence downhill towards another waymarked signpost, then cross a small wooden bridge and keep walking downhill past a third waymarked post. A narrow, grassy path descends to a small, shallow burn and then climbs to an electric fence. Keep to the edge of the field and walk along the path, following the white-capped posts of the electric fence as it ascends and descends round a steep gully to a wooden gate. The path maintains its course as it climbs to a wooden gate and a waymarked signpost at the base of **Downan Hill**. Turn left here and follow a grassy track which heads away from Downan Hill towards the coast, with fine views of Ballantrae signifying that the first port of call is near.

Continue along the path as it follows the course of a dry stone dyke, reaching two wooden gates at either side of a farm track just to the north of Downanhill Cottage. Once through the gates turn left onto a farm road and walk along it, passing through the substantial Langdale Farm and the smaller **Downan Farm**. The path then turns northeast to pass **Kinniegar Farm** to reach the road end. Turn left onto another road and walk along it, passing through the hamlet of **Garleffin** before the road joins the A77. Turn left here onto the pavement running beside the A77 with views towards the ruin of Ardstinchar Castle on the edge of the village of **Ballantrae**.

Ardstinchar Castle was built by Hugh Kennedy of Ardstinchar, a commander of Scottish troops who fought with Joan of Arc against English forces at the famous Siege of Orléans (1428-1429), an extremely significant battle of the Hundred Years' War in which Joan of Arc first established her renown. Thanks to his military prowess, Hugh was subsequently chosen to escort King Charles VII of France on a pilgrimage to the Holy Land. On his return the king bestowed upon him a knighthood and a substantial golden handshake that allowed him to purchase the land on which Ardstinchar Castle was built. It is said that Mary, Queen of Scots spent the night here in 1563.

The short walk along the pavement then crosses a bridge over the River Stinchar. ▶ The road passes **Ardstinchar Castle** and continues onto Ballantrae's Main Street, where the finish point of this route is reached at the small but perfectly formed Kennedy Mausoleum.

This bridge was built in 1964 but the older bridge, dating from 1770, can be seen a few yards further upriver.

Ballantrae was formed as a burgh in the 16th century, following the building of the castle here by the Kennedy family in the middle of the 15th. It translates from the Gaelic *Baile an Traighe* as 'the village on the shore' and its peaceful setting provides splendid views of the surrounding landscape and coast; it is a lovely place to spend some time. For many years Ballantrae was a fishing port, with smuggling commonplace along the coastline. Robert Louis Stevenson used the name of the village in his 1889 novel *The Master of Ballantrae*.

33

The compact but charming Kennedy Mausoleum

THE KENNEDY MAUSOLEUM

The Kennedy Mausoleum lies in the heart of the village and was built in 1604 by Lady Bargany. Her husband Gilbert Kennedy (who was Laird of Bargany) was killed in 1601 by the 5th Earl of Cassillis, John Kennedy, in an infamous incident that has since become known as 'The Maybole Snowballing'. Gilbert's funeral was apparently attended by over 1000 men on horseback and several dignitaries. He was subsequently buried at Ayr but when Lady Bargany died in 1605 both their bodies were taken to Ballantrae and laid to rest in the Kennedy Mausoleum. The graveyard also has some interesting gravestones, many of which commemorate those drowned at sea.

DAY 2
Ballantrae to Girvan

Start	Kennedy Mausoleum, Ballantrae NX 083 824
Finish	Girvan harbour NX 182 982
Distance	13 miles (21 km)
Time	5 hours
Maps	OS Landranger 76; OS Explorer 317 and 326
Terrain	Fairly flat using sandy and shingly beach, pavements, an old coach road and grass verge. However, there is one section that travels directly beside the busy A77 trunk road for a couple of miles where only a verge separates you from the road. Take great care here, especially if you are in a large group or with young children or dogs.
Refreshments	There is a shop and hotel in Ballantrae, a bistro at Lendalfoot and several shops, pubs and restaurants in Girvan.
Public Transport	Regular Stagecoach buses run between Girvan town centre and Ballantrae (see Appendix C). Girvan railway station (services including Ayr, Kilmarnock and Stranraer) is on Vicarton Street.

From Ballantrae the route heads down to the village's lovely harbour and onto a long stretch of sandy beach leading to Bennane Head (at one time the home of the notorious cannibal Sawney Bean). From here the path climbs directly beside the main A77 trunk road, which has to be crossed twice during the route so real care must be taken. The route descends into the quiet hamlet of Lendalfoot where a mixture of pavement and shore leads towards Kennedy's Pass and onto a superb old coach road that climbs high above the coast, providing magnificent views as well as being home to a variety of wildlife. It then drops back down to the coast and continues alongside the A77 into the busy town of Girvan using pavement, beach and promenade.

From the Kennedy Mausoleum turn left onto Main Street and then first left onto The Vennel. Walk along the pavement towards the shore, passing **Ballantrae Parish Church**, several houses and the primary school. On reaching a small car park the road sweeps round to the right and onto Foreland. ▶

Public toilets are available to the right of the car park.

Continue along Foreland on the pavement, passing Shore Road and Kintyre Avenue on your right until a small harbour is reached, where a waymarked sign points right to the slipway at the entrance of the harbour. Walk down the slipway and onto the sandy beach to continue north, heading away from **Ballantrae Bay** and towards Bennane Head. The beach provides good walking and the views towards Bennane Head, out to Ailsa Craig and back to Ballantrae are excellent.

As you approach two cottages at **Bennane Lea** turn right and walk towards a waymarked sign. At this point walk off the beach and onto a grassy track beside the cottages. Turn right to pass through a gate and cross an old road, then cross a cattle grid at another gate. Go through this gate to reach the very busy A77, which must be crossed. **Take great care here** as the traffic (including many trucks) moves along at the national speed limit of 60mph, making its way to and from the ferry ports at Cairnryan and Stranraer.

Once safely across turn left and climb steeply alongside the A77, walking on the grass verge between the metal barrier and the fence. This section of path travels

Ballantrae's fine, sandy beach leads all the way to Bennane Head

beside the road for approximately one mile and although there are several feet between you and the traffic real care must be taken, particularly if there is a large group, children or pets on the walk. As you gain height alongside the road the views back towards Ballantrae are superb. About halfway up the hill the metal barrier stops so take extra care here. Once at the top of the hill the houses of Bennane Lodge and **Meikle Bennane** are passed on the left, then as the A77 begins to descend the verge crosses a singletrack farm road (which leads to **Little Bennane**) and reaches a waymarked sign. Carefully cross the A77 here back onto the western side of the road.

map continues
on page 39

Near Bennane Head is a **cave** that runs to a depth of nearly 200m. Local legend states that this was the home of the infamous Alexander 'Sawney' Bean (spelt erroneously on the OS map as Sawny). He was the head of a Scottish family of

Looking back towards Ballantrae at dawn from Bennane Head

cannibals who reputedly murdered over 1000 men, women and children in the 15th or 16th century. The clan managed to keep their whereabouts secret for 25 years thanks to the cave being blocked by water at high tide, keeping its murderous inhabitants and the remains of their victims hidden from passers-by. It was only by chance that Sawney Bean and his band of outlaws were finally caught, when they ambushed a man and wife returning from a local fair. The husband put up a furious struggle with his sword and pistol, managing to escape (sadly his wife became the Bean family's final victim) and tell the magistrates at Glasgow. When King James VI was informed, he and an army of 400 men tracked the Beans down to their cave at Bennane Head. Following their capture, Sawney Bean and his clan were all executed without trial in Edinburgh.

Continue along the path as it descends alongside the A77 by way of a grass verge, which runs between a fence on the left and a metal barrier on the right that separates the path from the main road. The fence is there to protect against getting too close to the edge of the verge, as steep slopes fall away to the coast. The path here can be quite tight at times but the terrain is good for walking. Cross the entrance and exit of a small car park, then as you round a corner you are treated to superb views down to Lendalfoot, towards Pinbain Hill and further north to Turnberry.

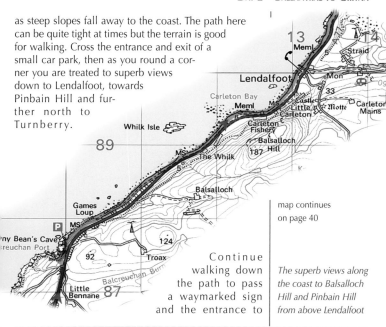

Continue walking down the path to pass a waymarked sign and the entrance to

The superb views along the coast to Balsalloch Hill and Pinbain Hill from above Lendalfoot

map continues on page 40

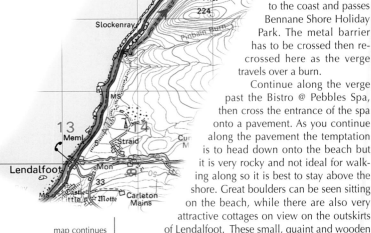

Balsalloch Farm and North Ballaird, before the route drops down to the coast and passes Bennane Shore Holiday Park. The metal barrier has to be crossed then re-crossed here as the verge travels over a burn.

Continue along the verge past the Bistro @ Pebbles Spa, then cross the entrance of the spa onto a pavement. As you continue along the pavement the temptation is to head down onto the beach but it is very rocky and not ideal for walking along so it is best to stay above the shore. Great boulders can be seen sitting on the beach, while there are also very attractive cottages on view on the outskirts of Lendalfoot. These small, quaint and wooden dwellings are quite idiosyncratic. As you approach Lendalfoot these views enhance the pleasant walking along the pavement. Bear left away from the A77 at a lay-by and follow the road round to the **Varyag Memorial**.

map continues on page 43

The **Varyag** was an iconic Russian warship that was badly damaged and suffered many casualties in the 1904 Battle of Chemulpo Bay during Russia's war with Japan. A mismatched battle heavily in favour of the Japanese resulted in extensive damage and the ship became immobile as a result. In 1905 she was salvaged by the Japanese and, renamed Soya, became part of their navy. During World War I, however, Japan became an ally and many ships were returned to Russia, including the Varyag in 1916. She was brought to Britain under her reclaimed Russian name in the following year for repairs but, because of civil war in Russia, they never took place. The ship was eventually sold as scrap to Germany in 1920 but, ironically, sank during a storm when being tugged across the Firth of Clyde. The Varyag went down only 450m off the coast at Lendalfoot.

When you leave the memorial continue along the road and back onto the pavement beside the A77. Head down onto the beach at this point where there is good solid walking by **Lendalfoot**. Once away from the village, however, make your way back up onto the pavement and onto a grass verge, as the beach becomes very rocky. Continue along the verge to pass the small, unobtrusive grave of one Archibald Hamilton and crew. The gravestone reads:

The Memory of Archibald Hamilton and crew, Natives of Kings Cross, Arran who were drowned near this place September 11th 1711.

Once away from the grave the verge becomes very narrow, so head back onto the beach. Continue over some boulders and onto a shingly beach that provides good walking with plentiful surrounding wildlife. As you walk along the beach you pass a sign to the right at the edge of

Climbing the old coach road away from Lendalfoot above Kennedy's Pass

the main road that informs road users that walkers cross the A77 after another 300 yards. At this point head back up to the road and onto the pavement, which then ends at a grass verge. Walk along the verge to reach a waymarked sign just before a bend in the road at **Slockenray**. Cross very carefully over to the eastern side of the road to reach a wooden gate. Go through the gate and climb a good path up a very steep slope away from Slockenray and onto an old 18th-century coach road. This steep-sided gorge is initially quite impressive but after the gravel path climbs steeply round a hairpin bend the gradient eases slightly. The pass runs high above the coast and gives fantastic views back to Bennane Head and Lendalfoot, as well as north along the coast and towards Arran.

The walking is excellent and very peaceful here, with a wide variety of surrounding wildlife including buzzards and kestrels.

Go through a wooden gate and follow a good track, climbing gradually towards the lower slopes of **Pinbain Hill**. ◀ As the track levels out at the base of the hill, go through another wooden gate. Continue on the track, traversing the hill's lower slopes. The hill climbs steeply to your right with sheep grazing on the open moorland.

The track continues through another two gates towards the ruin of **Kilranny cottage**, which has a **radio mast** to its left. At the cottage go through another three gates and walk round the perimeter of the house on a boggy track. After the cottage a stony track then begins to descend steeply back down towards the coast, with good views towards Girvan and, further north, Turnberry. Here the track runs alongside open farmland and walkers should be vigilant during lambing season. ◀ After

If you have a dog with you ensure that it is on a lead and kept under control.

another wooden gate the track descends towards the road and turns sharply to the left. However, ignore this turning. Instead, follow the track straight on at a waymarked sign onto a muddy track that continues its course along the base of the higher ground rising to the right. There will be livestock in the field here at certain times of the year. The good, level track continues with the A77 to the left and then passes a lovely waterfall that is some 25–30ft in height. Go through a gate and walk towards the buildings at **Ardwell Farm**. Just before reaching the farm the track sweeps round to the left and down to the A77.

Carefully cross the road here, then turn right onto a broad grass verge and walk alongside the A77 for 300m. You pass Ardwell Farm on the right to reach **Ardwell Bay**, where there is a whitewashed cottage on the right-hand side of the road. Pass the cottage and turn left onto a track that leads down onto the beach. The shingly beach here provides good walking and gives great views to the northwest of Arran, Ailsa Craig and Kintyre, inland to the broad flanks of Byne Hill and further up the coast towards Girvan. Continue to walk along the beach where lovely big boulders pepper the sand and ducks, seagulls, herring gulls and oystercatchers can be seen along the shore.

The beach continues to **Black Neuk** but before a short section of sea wall is reached walk back up to the

A horse cools off on a hot summer's evening at Woodland Bay near Girvan

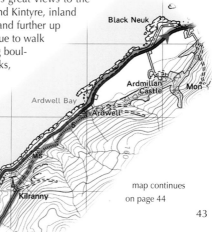

map continues on page 44

43

pavement at the roadside. Walk along the pavement towards **Woodland Bay** where, again, the temptation is to head back to the beach but when the tide is out the amount of seaweed the sea leaves behind does not make for pleasant walking. The pavement then joins a short section of old road that runs parallel to the A77. Walk along here to reach a grass verge at the A77 opposite Woodland Farm. Turn left here and walk along the broad verge past **Woodland Farm** (which is also a hotel and has a shop and restaurant). Here the verge gives way to a pavement. Continue on, until you reach a very narrow section of footpath that is separated from the A77 only by a crash barrier. Carefully walk along this section, which continues for 120m.

After this section head back down onto the beach, which takes you away from the main road and provides good walking towards **Girvan**. Continue to walk along the beach to reach a grassy path that skirts the edge of Ainslie Manor Nursing Home and leads back onto the pavement at a waymarked sign on the outskirts of the town. Turn left here and walk along the pavement, through a car park and into Ainslie Park to join Girvan promenade. Walk along the promenade (which runs parallel with Edmiston Drive) or along the beach, which is to the left of the promenade. Walking along the promenade to Girvan's harbour makes for a lovely way to end the day's walk.

There have been people living within the area for around 5000 years but it was not until 1668 that the town of **Girvan** was established. A charter granted by King Charles II in that year gave the right for a harbour and fort to be built, with added privileges such as fortnightly markets. A planned rebuilding of the town began in the 18th century, when textile manufacturing became predominant in the town and more people moved to the area as a result. The attractive harbour, which sits at the mouth of the River Girvan, has always been the town's focal point and it is still a working harbour today. An RNLI lifeboat station and the town's coastguard station are located beside the harbour and many day-trippers visit Girvan to enjoy its seaside location.

Fishing trawlers leave and enter the harbour at Girvan every day

DAY 3

Girvan to Dunure

Start	Girvan harbour NX 182 982
Finish	Dunure harbour NS 253 158
Distance	14 miles (23 km)
Time	6 hours
Maps	OS Landranger 76 and 70; OS Explorer 326
Terrain	There is a variety in this section including coastal paths, farm roads, pavements and fields as well as some sections across beach and golf course. Part of the route also goes through Culzean Country Park. There are a few burns to be crossed en route, which at high tide may result in wet feet. It is best to consult a tide timetable before starting this walk.
Refreshments	Girvan has several shops, pubs and restaurants. Turnberry, Maidens and Dunure all have hotels (see Appendix B). Culzean Country Park has a restaurant with seasonal opening hours.
Public Transport	Girvan railway station (services including Ayr, Kilmarnock and Stranraer) is on Vicarton Street. There is no direct bus service between Dunure and Girvan. Smith's Coaches provide a service from Dunure to Ayr and then a connecting bus is required between Ayr and Girvan. See Appendix C for details.

From Girvan a walk round the harbour heads towards Turnberry by way of farm tracks, coastal paths and beach. There are a couple of burns to be crossed along the way, which at high tide may be problematic. Like much of this route the journey to Turnberry is lovely and quiet with great birdlife to spot such as razorbills and oystercatchers. The final couple of miles are superb; the beautiful sandy beach striking its course beside the enormous, glorious dunes heading towards the magnificent Turnberry Lighthouse and giving exceptional views across the Firth of Clyde to Arran. Via the world-renowned Turnberry golf course the route then passes through Maidens and heads into the peaceful surrounds of Culzean Country Park, passing the truly magnificent Culzean Castle. A long stretch of beach then leads to Croy, where (if you arrive at high tide) a short, unavoidable stretch of coastline at Isle Port will be underwater. This either has to be negotiated at high tide (which is possible but your legs will get wet) or crossed when the tide has receded. It is recommended that you check the tide timetables before walking this section. A path then climbs high above the coastline across open farmland before descending into Dunure.

From the harbour at **Girvan** walk through the car park alongside it and continue onto Knockcushan Street. Walk along with the harbour and River Girvan to your left, pass the **RNLI Lifeboat Station** and continue along the pavement towards the town centre. At a set of traffic lights at the corner of Knockcushan Street and Dalrymple Street turn left into Bridge Street. Walk along the pavement past some shops and then bear left at a waymarked signpost into Threadneedle Crescent.

Follow the pavement along Threadneedle Crescent and when opposite the entrance to a caravan park turn left and cross the bridge over the River Girvan, then turn left again into Newton Kennedy and walk along the pavement towards the harbour. At a boatyard turn right and

Working boats and pleasure craft still use the harbour at Girvan

47

You are now on the opposite side of the harbour.

continue along Newton Kennedy. ◄ Walk past the coast-guard station and then turn left onto a cycle path, which provides flat walking alongside the river towards the end of the harbour. Ahead of you now rises the unmistakeable outline of Ailsa Craig.

The cycle path continues above the shore through grassy parkland towards **Girvan golf course**. Just before the small car park at the golf course starter's hut, the path turns to the right towards Golf Course Road. Take this path to cross the road and then turn right at a waymarked signpost into a side street. Walk along it and at the end turn left onto a singletrack road. Confusingly, this is still Golf Course Road.

Walk along Golf Course Road (there is no pavement), passing the back gardens of a row of houses on the left and with the River Girvan to your right. At the end of the houses pass the 9th tee of the golf course, then continue along the road as it heads away from Girvan alongside the golf course with farmland to the left and some good views of the high hills above the town on the right. The road then sweeps away from the golf course past some cottages and continues with a railway track to the right. Once past an industrial site the road gives way to another minor road at a waymarked sign.

Turn left here to head towards the busy A77 and at the junction with the A77 cross the minor road and turn left into **Girvan Mains Farm**. The route passes through the main courtyard of this busy working farm and so great care and consideration should be taken and dogs must be kept on their leads. Walk through the courtyard, which merges with a singletrack road, to continue away from the farm. ◄ Pass three cottages and walk along the path beside a dry stone dyke. Once past the cottages the road sweeps round to the right and continues just above the beach with great views towards Turnberry.

The farm road provides easy walking and passes **Girvan Waste Water Treatment Works** to reach a way-marked post. Bear left here onto an indistinct path that leads down onto the shore. Follow the grassy track along a raised beach with farmland to the right, separated from

This section can be muddy as it heads towards the coast.

the track by a wall. The going underfoot can be rough at times but the path remains obvious.

As you approach a line of cottages the path merges with a wider track and continues along the raised beach. Just before the cottages there is a signpost informing you of a diversion path, which can be used if the tide is too high to walk along the beach. If this is the case then go through the gate and turn left keeping to the edge of a field. ▶ Walk along the path (which passes behind the cottages), cross a singletrack road and, when the last cottage is behind you, continue to a gate at a waymarked sign and turn left back down onto the beach.

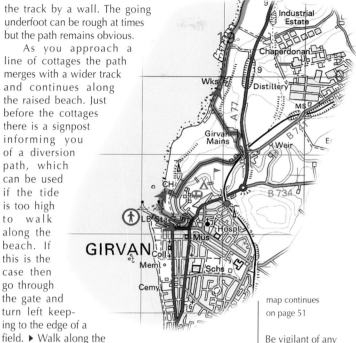

map continues on page 51

Be vigilant of any livestock and careful not to damage any crops.

If, however, the tide is low enough to walk along the beach then turn left away from the gate and signpost and walk down onto the shore and along the soft sand past a large sea defence wall and the cottages sitting above it. The beach offers pleasant walking but, again, if the tide is very high then the stony ground at the top of the beach may have to be used, which may slightly slow your progress.

Continue along the beach towards **Dipple** shore and the **alginate factory**. Just before the factory is the out-flow to Lady Burn, which (again at high tide) can prove

Turnberry Lighthouse was built in 1873 and holds a prominent position above Turnberry Point

problematic to cross. Even at lower tides your feet may get a little wet. Cross the burn, pass the factory and walk along the shore on softer sand beside sea defences. The shore comprises sand, seaweed, shingle, stones and boulders and, again, at very high tides progress may be slow here. 200m past the factory a signpost to the right of the beach highlights an access track to **Dowhill Farm**, which has a shop and restaurant. An optional short detour along this track takes you to the farm.

Continue along the beach with good, firm sand underfoot, passing **Dowhill Port** and crossing a narrow outflow. At an old fisherman's hut another outflow has to be crossed, which, again, may mean your feet get wet. As **Turnberry** is approached the walking is excellent. It is a beautiful beach with the iconic **Turnberry Lighthouse** pulling you on. The dunes are spectacular, reaching about 25ft in height. As you approach Milton Burn the equally impressive **Turnberry Hotel** comes into view. Milton Burn will pose problems for crossing, even at lower tides, and you may well have to take your boots off to cross.

Occupying a spectacular position above Turnberry Point, the whitewashed brick walls of **Turnberry Lighthouse** can be seen for many miles. It was built to the plans of the pioneering lighthouse designer Thomas Stevenson (father of the famous author Robert Louis Stevenson) in 1873 and was erected on the site of the former Turnberry Castle. Some of the remains of the castle can still be seen here. Robert the Bruce's father owned the castle and it is known that he spent his childhood here. Some sources contend that Turnberry Castle was also the birthplace of the future King of Scots in 1274.

If any provisions are needed at this point, cross the burn and take the path to the right of the beach at a waymarked sign. This leads over **Turnberry golf course** and towards the **post office**. If not then after crossing Milton Burn walk along the beach towards **Turnberry Point**, where there is an obvious path beneath the lighthouse that runs through the dunes. A sign makes you aware that as walkers you are using the route at your own risk; keep off the greens and respect golfers' etiquette.

map continues on page 53

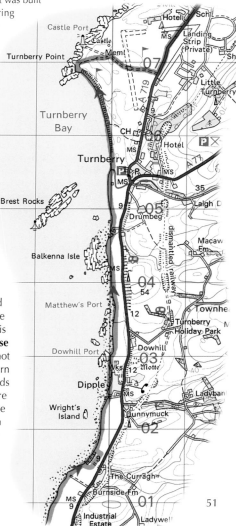

51

The world-renowned **Turnberry golf course** was established in 1901 and, five years later, **Turnberry Hotel** opened for business. Both have been incredibly popular tourist destinations ever since, even after the railway line that served the area (dubbed 'the golfer's line' as it served so many courses along the Ayrshire coast) was closed in 1942. The RAF used some of the course's land as an airbase and landing strip during World War One while during World War Two the hotel was converted into a military hospital.

The golf course is one of the world's best. Surprisingly, it did not hold its first Open Championship until 1977, when Tom Watson and Jack Nicklaus played out their memorable 'Duel in the Sun'. Having had identical scores throughout each of the first three rounds of the competition they were tied right up until the 16th hole in the fourth and final round. Watson then birdied the final two holes on the Sunday to complete a famous victory. The last hole on the course has since been renamed 'Duel in the Sun' to commemorate the contest between the two on the final day.

Leave the beach and walk along the path through the dunes to climb gradually towards the golf course. At the top of the path turn right onto the golf course itself at the back of the 8th green. Walk around the back of the green (keep quiet and wait until any golfers have finished playing before moving) to reach a sign pointing straight on. ◀ There is also a lot of surrounding wildlife like stonechats and linnets, particularly in spring when the gorse bushes give off an amazing coconut aroma. The fairway gives way to a singletrack road. Walk along it through the golf course to meet with another singletrack road. Turn right and walk down this road through the golf course to the road end. Pass through a wooden gate, turn left onto the A719 and walk along the pavement towards **Maidens**.

Here the views towards Maidens, Turnberry Lighthouse and the golf course are superb.

The full title of the village is the Maidens of Turnberry and the bulk of it is centred around the small, attractive harbour that sits on the southern end of Maidenhead Bay.

After spending the winter of 1306 in a castle on Rathlin Island off the coast of County Antrim in Northern Ireland, **Maidens** is where King Robert the Bruce arrived back in Scotland. Rathlin Island and its castle had provided him with refuge after being defeated by the English at Perth earlier in 1306 and here he planned his return to Scotland.

Maidens harbour may not be as busy as it once was but it still has some attractive boats

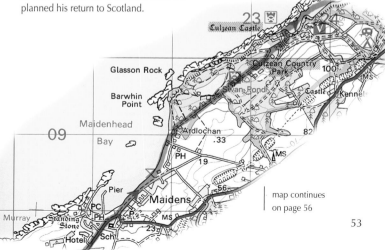

map continues on page 56

53

Go past the Malin Court Hotel and then descend down into Maidens, crossing Baineshill Drive. Cross Harbour Road and then walk across the open parkland (keeping the harbour to your left) towards the shore to reach a waymarked sign. Here a narrow concrete path continues at the left edge of the park above **Maidenhead Bay** and passes a line of houses and a caravan park on the right. The paved path ends and then continues over grass towards a car park. At the car park turn left down a track onto the beach.

Turn right and walk along the beach towards the woods of Culzean Country Park. Pass sea defences, a cottage and a caravan park to meet a river. At this point turn right and follow the edge of the beach to a wooden footbridge. Cross the bridge and then turn right into **Culzean Country Park**.

A good path climbs gradually through the woods to an old cottage, before bearing left to reach two old gateposts. It then immediately turns right to pass a National Trust donation box and continues to climb gradually through Culzean Country Park. Continue along the long, straight path, which goes through some lovely woodland containing lots of plants and animals. ◄ The

You may catch a glimpse of squirrels or roe deer here.

path then passes a lovely brick cottage on the right to reach an overflow car park beside a wooden cottage to the left. Here the path becomes a singletrack road that passes the car park to reach a pavement. Climb uphill through mixed woodland, passing the **Swan Pond** and another overflow car park. The pavement then climbs quite steeply and goes by Culzean's Walled Garden and an estate house. Cross a minor road at the end of the Walled Garden and walk down towards the main country park road. The pavement then sweeps round to the right and continues beside the main road to a waymarked sign. Turn left here and descend alongside the road towards **Culzean Castle**. Go by the main car park and, just before the Information Centre and shop, bear left onto a path that leads through an archway underneath the castle entrance. Once through the archway a path to the left leads up to the Castle grounds.

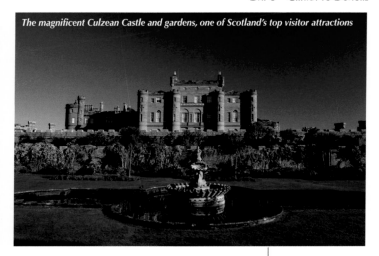

The magnificent Culzean Castle and gardens, one of Scotland's top visitor attractions

CULZEAN CASTLE

Culzean Country Park, which became Scotland's first country park in 1969, is run by the National Trust for Scotland and has over 600 acres of gardens and woodland as well as three miles of coastline within its boundaries. At its heart is the magnificent centrepiece Culzean Castle, a truly awe-inspiring building with a cliff-top position that adds to its grandeur. The castle had inauspicious beginnings, being no more than a stone tower house in the 12th century. Its expansion into the sumptuous building that exists today began in 1776 and was designed by the great architect Robert Adam at the behest of David Kennedy, the 10th Earl of Cassillis. The superb walled gardens were also built around this time and these were originally kitchen gardens that provided food for the castle's inhabitants.

When the Kennedy family donated Culzean to the National Trust of Scotland in 1945 they asked that General Eisenhower be given an apartment within Culzean Castle in recognition of his role during the Second World War as Supreme Commander of the Allied Forces in Europe. Eisenhower then visited the castle on four occasions, including once when President. Nowadays the Eisenhower Apartment is available as accommodation for visitors and Culzean Castle is one of Scotland's top visitor attractions.

Culzean Castle holds an incredibly commanding position above Culzean Bay

To continue on the Ayrshire Coastal Path walk straight on and then either follow a steep path or descend by two flights of wooden steps down towards the shore. Go through two large concrete gateposts, pass the Gas Manager's House Exhibition of William Murdoch (a pioneer of the gas industry who was born in the Ayrshire village of

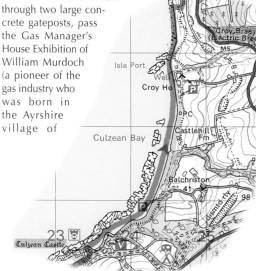

map continues on page 60

Lugar) and follow the path down onto **Culzean Bay**. A narrow strip of beach with wooded slopes rising steeply to the right leads away from Culzean Castle Country Park. Walk along the soft sand and enjoy the excellent, dramatic views back towards the castle. The path then climbs over a rocky outcrop, taking you momentarily above the shore, and then drops back down to continue past a cottage and alongside mixed woodland. The beach curves its way along the coast but it can be stony and narrow at times. At very high tides walking is confined to the top of the beach, which slows progress.

Walk along the beach towards Croy, passing a few cottages and a concrete slipway that leads to a small car park. Cross an outflow, which is made possible by a couple of large flat stones, and continue by **Croy House** and the large sea defences towards the slipway at Croyburnfoot Caravan Park.

Do not go up the slipway, as both the road leading to Croy House and the caravan park are private property. Instead walk along the beach towards **Isle Port**, climbing over a row of boulders and passing the caravan park. Depending on the height of the tide when you

Climbing above Croy, the path provides superb views along the coast towards Dunure

Again, check the tide times before walking this section.

reach Isle Port, you may have to go barefoot. It is a very short section of rocky outcrop that is impassable at very high tide until the tide recedes. Even at lower tides it may be best to take off your boots to get past. ◄

Once past Isle Port walk along the big flat shelves of rock onto a shingly shore and continue along it towards the high ground at the end of the beach. This stretch is well away from any roads and is therefore quiet with great views of Arran and a good selection of birdlife including black-headed gulls and oystercatchers. At the end of the beach follow an obvious path through the dunes to a waymarked sign. Turn right and climb steeply up a grassy track that zigzags away from the coast and climbs high above the shore to give superb views all round. Go through a gate at the top of the hill, leading into an open field. Stick to the field edge (as there is open farmland to the right) and descend gradually along a narrow path, keeping the fence to your left. The fence separates the path from steep cliffs that fall sharply to the shore.

The path descends to a footbridge, crosses a burn and then goes through a gate to continue round the field edge alongside the fence. The path then follows the natural direction of the land to head away from the coast above a deep gorge and reaches the head of the gorge at a way-marked sign. Turn left here, cross a stile and then descend a flight of wooden steps to a shallow burn. Cross the burn then turn left and follow the line of the fence back towards the coast. It then climbs gradually, passing an old coast-guard tower, to reach a gate below a **radio mast** at the top of the field beside Castle Road. Go through the gate then descend a grassy path that runs parallel to Castle Road towards **Dunure**.

The picturesque village of **Dunure** is built around its small harbour and is home to a small number of working fishing boats. The harbour was improved in 1811 by the Earl of Cassillis and for a time it was another of the industrious fishing ports along Scotland's west coast.

There are good views of Dunure Castle as the narrow path continues high above the coast (at the time of writing saplings had recently been planted here). Walk down the path, which can be boggy and steep at some points. It then levels out and merges with wider track as it begins to climb towards Kennedy Park and Dunure. As you enter Kennedy Park pick up a tarmac path and then turn left onto a path leading down towards **Dunure Castle**.

DUNURE CASTLE

Dunure Castle was the original base of the Kennedy Clan and it has a fascinating history. Although hard to believe today (owing to its derelict nature) for several hundred years from the 12th century it was more important than its neighbour at Culzean. In 1563 Mary, Queen of Scots stayed here for three nights as a guest of Gilbert Kennedy, the 4th Earl of Cassillis as she made one of her many tours of the country. The castle's magnificent vantage point overlooking the Firth of Clyde to Arran's serrated profile provided the Kennedys with an easily defendable position and an excellent lookout post. As the Kennedys' position of power and wealth grew the castle was accordingly expanded, with many rooms being added to the original building, including a prison.

The prison has a very dark past, dominated by the infamous account of The Roasting of Allan Stewart. Following a long dispute with Gilbert, the 4th Earl of Cassillis, concerning who had the ownership rights to the lands of nearby Crossraguel Abbey (Queen Mary had appointed Stewart abbot in 1565 and with that came possession of the surrounding lands, but Gilbert had previously come to an agreement with the prior abbot, his own uncle, to lease the land), Stewart was captured by the Earl and led into Dunure's ominously titled Black Vault. Here the captive was stripped, bound and slowly cooked over a large, open fire until he agreed to sign over the lands of the abbey. However, the gruesome tale did not end there. After a week or so, in which time Stewart (with untreated wounds) was still imprisoned, it came to light that his first signature was invalid due to there being no witness to it. Therefore Gilbert demanded he sign the deeds again before a witness. At first Stewart refused but after he was strung up and roasted again, he succumbed (under unimaginable levels of pain and suffering) and signed the lands over to the Earl.

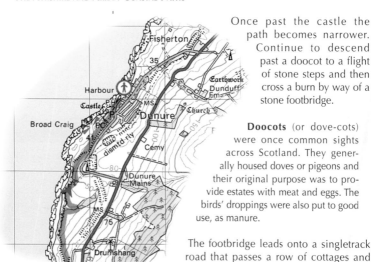

Once past the castle the path becomes narrower. Continue to descend past a doocot to a flight of stone steps and then cross a burn by way of a stone footbridge.

Doocots (or dove-cots) were once common sights across Scotland. They generally housed doves or pigeons and their original purpose was to provide estates with meat and eggs. The birds' droppings were also put to good use, as manure.

The footbridge leads onto a singletrack road that passes a row of cottages and down to **Dunure harbour**.

Although hard to believe now, for several hundred years Dunure Castle was more important than its neighbour at Culzean

DAY 4

Dunure to Troon

Start	Dunure harbour NS 253 158
Finish	Troon promenade NS 328 298
Distance	18 miles (29 km)
Time	7 hours
Maps	OS Landranger 70; OS Explorer 326
Terrain	Sandy and rocky beaches, farm roads, fields, cycle tracks, pavements and beach promenade cover the longest section of the Ayrshire Coastal Path. There are a few sections where high tides could obstruct the route.
Refreshments	Dunure, Alloway, Ayr, Prestwick and Troon all have a wide selection of shops, restaurants, pubs and hotels (see Appendix B). Alloway also has an excellent restaurant at the recently renovated Robert Burns Birthplace Museum.
Public Transport	There is no direct bus service between Troon and Dunure. Regular buses and trains run between Troon and Ayr; Smith's Coaches provide a service between Ayr and Dunure (see Appendix C for details). Troon railway station (services including Ayr, Kilmarnock and Glasgow) is on Barassie Street.

From Dunure sandy beaches and grassy tracks lead to rockier stretches of beach beneath great cliffs. Just before Bracken Bay a steep pull climbs high above the shore along field edges and onto the line of an old railway track, which has exceptional views towards the Heads of Ayr. Good paths then descend back to the shore from where a lovely long stretch of sandy beach culminates at Greenan shore. The path then moves away from the coast into Alloway to reach the Robert Burns Birthplace Museum and Burns Cottage, where the life of Scotland's Bard, who was born in Alloway, is celebrated. Leaving Alloway a promenade then runs above the shore into Ayr passing some of the royal burgh's wonderful historic sites. On leaving Ayr, a combination of beach and dunes take you into Prestwick, passing its renowned golf course (where the very first Open Championship was played) and then a final, long walk along beautiful sandy beaches concludes on Troon promenade. There are several sections where high tides may come into play so remember to check the tide timetables beforehand.

Leave Dunure by walking anti-clockwise round the harbour and then, passing a waymarked sign on the wall, drop left down onto the beach. The shingly beach passes Dunure House and runs beneath a sea wall. Walk along soft sand and head for an obvious gap in the rocks at the end of the beach. At the gap follow a narrow path through the rocks at a waymarked sign to continue down to a wooden gate.

Go through the gate and then immediately bear right at a daubed white mark on a rock. Continue up the hill and follow a narrow path, climbing gradually away from the beach to avoid a very rocky section. At the top of the slope the path bears left and runs parallel above the coast, following an indistinct grassy path along an open field with the houses of **Fisherton** above. There may be livestock in these fields at certain times of the year, so dogs should be kept on their leads at all times. Continue through the field passing more white daubed marks and enjoy the good views along the rugged coast towards Ayr and Troon.

Stick to the main path along the left of the field, which becomes more prominent as you

There are no roads or paths here and it is very peaceful.

progress. ◄ Once past a waymarked sign bear left along a grassy path back down towards the shore. Walk along the soft sandy beach and then bear right onto another

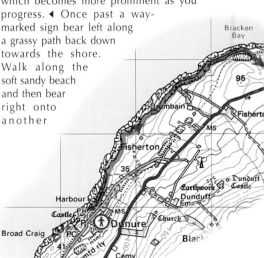

map continues
on page 64

grassy track that continues slightly above the shore. The path peters out but continue to walk parallel with the coastline along the water's edge until you meet a dry stone dyke and a stile. Go over the stile, then immediately cross a narrow burn. Walk along a raised beach on an obvious path through gorse with higher ground to the right.

The path climbs gradually to a waymarked sign. Drop down left here, descending a short, steep section of boggier ground to a beach below **Drumbain**. ▶ Walk along the shore, which has steep cliffs rising to the right and lovely views towards Arran. It is advisable to walk along the top of the beach, as the lower reaches are strewn with boulders.

The boulders then become unavoidable as you are hemmed in by cliffs to the right and the water's edge to the left and so make your way carefully along this short section. Again, there are no other roads or paths into this area. An abundance of birdlife is on view here including shags, herons and oystercatchers.

Cross a burn underneath a lovely small waterfall and then meander your way round a small cove through the boulders towards **Bracken Bay** and onto a shingly

There are great views back to Dunure Castle and Ailsa Craig

At high tides the beach may be impassable until the water recedes and there is no alternative route.

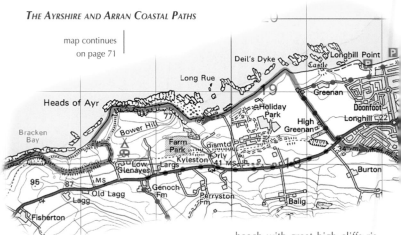

map continues
on page 71

beach with great high cliffs rising to the right. At this point a very indistinct path climbs away from the shore and up into the cliffs, leading above Bracken Bay. This path is very easy to miss and it is not waymarked, so keep your eyes peeled for it. Climb up the steep narrow path to reach a line of wooden steps, which continue to a wooden gate. Go through the gate and then turn left and descend gradually along the field edge, following the line of white-topped fence posts. This section travels high above the shore and provides superb views, particularly towards the Heads of Ayr. Follow the field edge to reach another gate. Pass through it and continue to walk round the field, climbing to another gate that leads out of the field and onto a flat, broad track. This track travels above the line of an old railway and there are more stunning views here.

The track gives good flat walking and eventually joins the route of the railway line as it continues above Bracken Bay. Go through another gate and follow the track as it continues above the fields on either side. Before a caravan park is reached descend to the right to a gate. Go through it and then cross a farm road. Climb left back up onto the track to continue towards the caravan park.

Just before the caravan park the track narrows to a path and bears left at a waymarked sign to drop down to a field edge and a fence. Pass through two wooden gates and continue straight on past a line of caravans. Go through another gate, turn left and walk away from the caravan park along the field edge back towards the coast.

A good wide track now runs alongside a fence over open farmland to another gate. Go through it onto a narrow track that is fenced in on both sides, descend down to the eastern end of Bracken Bay and then gradually down onto the beach. Here turn right and walk towards the **Heads of Ayr**. The beach has good firm sand to walk along as you approach the great cliffs at the Heads of Ayr but be aware that this section would cause problems at higher tides. Walk underneath the impressive cliffs and over a rocky shelf with great erratic boulders on the shore. As you round the corner there are great views towards Greenan Castle and Ayr.

John Kennedy of Baltersan built **Greenan Castle** in the early 1600s on the site of an ancient fort. It was built as a basic tower house with a courtyard and outbuildings. Today, only the main structure survives, balancing perilously on the edge of the cliffs above the shore.

Ayr and Greenan Castle from the Heads of Ayr

65

Greenan Castle dates from the early 1600s and holds a commanding position above the shore

Once past the shelf walk along a sandier beach and continue towards a **holiday park**. Again, high tide would be a problem here and it would have to recede before progress could be made. Alternatively, it may be possible to walk carefully along the uneven, boulder-strewn ground at the top of the shore. At low tide the walking is very pleasant.

Continue on the beach as it sweeps round to the left and cross a narrow burn. Just before reaching the holiday park climb from the beach onto a wide track to walk along with the park now on your right. The path then continues onto a broad grassy verge. Bear left here to drop back down onto the beach.

Walk along the sandy beach to reach **Deil's Dyke**, which is a high rounded sand dune. Bear right from the beach onto an obvious path that climbs through the dunes and onto a narrow path. Walk along the path as it continues high above Greenan shore and gives great views towards the castle, which is precariously positioned on the cliffs. As the path then descends steeply down towards Greenan shore stay on the path and continue through the dunes to meet with a waymarked sign for Burns Cottage.

Turn right here onto a broad farm track that climbs gradually away from the shore, passing Greenan Cottage to join a singletrack road (which is also a cycle track). The road is flat and straight, with great views towards the Carrick Hills. It then begins to climb gradually, passing the impressive house of **High Greenan**. When the road sweeps round to the left turn right onto a path at a waymarked sign and walk along to meet the A719. Carefully cross the busy road onto the pavement opposite, then turn left and cross the minor road leading to **Burton Farm**. Bear right onto a cycle path and walk along it away from the A719.

Continue along this peaceful, flat track on the outskirts of Alloway through pleasant mixed woodland, passing several impressive houses. ▶ This track continues into **Alloway**, passing beneath a bridge and then crossing the red brick bridge high above the River Doon where there are good views along the river towards the **Auld Brig o' Doon**. Once past Mungo's Well (an old spring that now flows into a small concrete basin) the track continues beneath a lengthy underpass. At the end a path turns 180° away from the main track. Climb this path to reach Murdoch's Lone opposite the Robert Burns Birthplace Museum. The museum re-opened in December 2010 after a major £21 million refurbishment and now contains an amazing array of artefacts and memorabilia linked to the poet (the OS map is yet to be updated from the museum's previous name: the Tam o' Shanter Experience). Well worth a visit, its entrance is across the road and up ahead.

There are good views here over open farmland towards the Carrick Hills.

ROBERT BURNS AND ALLOWAY

The lovely village of Alloway is the birthplace of Scotland's national bard, Robert Burns, and the name of the village has since become inextricably linked with that of the country's most famous son. Born to humble beginnings here on the 25th of January 1759, his work is now renowned across the globe with *Tam o' Shanter*, *Ae Fond Kiss* and *Auld Lang Syne* (sung worldwide every Hogmanay) some of his best-known works. There are several interesting places to visit within Alloway including the Burns Monument, which lies within the park. The monument was opened to the

Burns Cottage, the birthplace of Scotland's national bard, Robert Burns

public in 1823 after the money to build it was raised by local admirers of Burns. Near the monument and crossing the River Doon is the Brig o' Doon, which was chosen by Burns as the setting of the finale to *Tam o' Shanter*. The brig is used as a backdrop to many paintings of the area.

The old kirkyard in the village is also worth a visit. It dates from around the 16th century and has a number of old gravestones including that of William Burnes, Robert Burns' father. Despite much speculation it remains unclear why the poet chose to spell the surname differently and there is, as yet, no definitive account. One theory is that the pronunciation was the same and Robert simply decided to drop the extra letter; another relates to a legal battle William had regarding alleged unpaid arrears to the estate holder for his farm. William won the case but was left in debt because of it, so when he died Robert and his brother Gilbert decided to alter the spelling to distance themselves from associations with this bad debt. To add to the confusion, William's gravestone in the kirkyard has the spelling Burns.

A visit to Alloway would not be complete without visiting **Burns Cottage**, where the poet was born. Built in 1757 by his father, this beautiful thatched roof cottage was home to Robert Burns for the first seven years of his life and is now a magnificent museum run by the National Trust.

To continue, cross the wooden bridge directly opposite the museum then turn left onto a paved path, which swings right past a huge mouse sculpture (a reference to one of Robert Burns' finest poems *To a Mouse*). The path runs parallel with the B7024 alongside some lovely weather vanes, which reference more of Burns' most iconic works. Follow the path to reach the road. Carefully cross here and turn right then left onto Greenfield Avenue. ▶

Walk down Greenfield Avenue through the leafy suburbs of Alloway to reach the A719. Cross the road at a waymarked sign and take the singletrack road straight ahead that runs down to the right of a shop. Follow the track, which passes through hedgerows and alongside the River Doon, past a fishermen's bothy to reach a bridge. Turn right here and walk along the path onto the esplanade that runs above the long, sandy beach of **Seafield** towards **Ayr**.

To visit Burns Cottage, continue on past the junction with Greenfield Avenue. The cottage is further along the road, past a car park on the left.

Ayr, the county town of Ayrshire, was granted royal burgh status in 1205, eight years after King William the Lion founded a castle here. The town was at one stage called Inverayr, which derived from the Gaelic *Inbhir Air* meaning 'mouth of the river Ayr', before dropping the prefix. It has played a major part in Scottish history over the years. Robert the Bruce held the first Parliament of Scotland in Ayr in 1315. In 1652 Oliver Cromwell built a fortress for his men here, much of which can still be seen today. John Loudon McAdam, the renowned engineer, was born in Ayr in 1756. He developed a process he called 'macadamisation', which was the building of roads using crushed stone and gravel on top of a base of larger stones. When tar was added to his original idea to cope with the rise of the motor car in the early 20th century, his name lived on with the birth of Tarmacadam.

For centuries, Ayr's harbour was one of the most important on the west coast of Scotland. Wool, linen and fish have all been crucial trades in the town's development. Today Ayr has a population of around 50,000 and is an extremely interesting and attractive place to visit. Its long beach and accessibility to Glasgow means it is also popular with day-trippers.

Continue along the esplanade, which gives good, flat walking towards Ayr as it passes a large **car park**. At a small roundabout and a waymarked sign turn right into Blackburn Drive and then left onto a path that makes its way through the open parkland of Low Green. At the end of Low Green cross Pavilion Road onto Wellington Square and walk along the pavement, passing the impressive Sheriff Court.

> **Wellington Square** was built in 1806 in honour of Arthur Wellesley, the 1st Duke of Wellington, one of the major political and military luminaries of his time. He defeated Napoleon at the Battle of Waterloo in 1815 and became UK Prime Minister in 1828. There are several fine Georgian villas lining the square as well as the striking Sheriff Court. Within the square itself is Ayr cenotaph and several statues, including that of Archibald Montgomerie, the 13th Earl of Eglinton, a British politician who became Lord Lieutenant of Ireland twice in the 1850s.

Once past Wellington Square cross Bath Place into Cassillis Street and walk along the pavement, crossing Charlotte Street Lane and passing some large houses. Cross Charlotte Street and, as you continue along Cassillis Street, turn right onto Bruce Crescent to reach St John's Tower.

> The **tower** is all that remains of the Church of St John. Robert the Bruce held the first meeting of the Scottish Parliament here, the year after his famous 1314 victory over Edward II's English army at Bannockburn. It is assumed that John Knox, leader of the Protestant Reformation, preached here (his son-in-law was the church's minister from 1600-1606) and it is thought that Knox's daughter, Elizabeth, is buried beside the tower. The town council demolished the tower in 1726 but it was restored by Lord Bute in 1914, who transferred the ownership of the tower to the Burgh of Ayr in 1949.

Pass St John's Tower to continue onto Montgomerie Terrace, which (after passing some tennis courts) sweeps round to the left and merges into Seabank Road to lead towards the esplanade. Just before reaching the esplanade turn right and then right again onto a cobbled street that heads away from the coast towards Ayr town centre. Continue past the remains of Cromwell's citadel and a replica cannon to reach the end of the road.

map continues on page 75

Turn right onto South Harbour Street and walk along the pavement above the River Ayr, passing a restaurant and some pubs.

Cross Fort Street and continue along South Harbour Street into a small courtyard called Boat Vennel, which used to be the main route through the town to the harbour and is home to Loudoun Hall.

Loudoun Hall is the oldest building in Ayr. It dates from the early 15th century and is an important example of a townhouse of that era. Built by the merchant and former Provost of Ayr, James Tait, it was owned for many years by the Campbells of Loudoun, who were the Sheriffs of Ayrshire. Over the years it fell into disrepair until it was saved by John Crichton-Stuart, the 4th Marquis of Bute, and restored during the 1940s.

At the end of Boat Vennel turn left into New Bridge Street (to the right is Sandgate, which where you will find many shops as well as the tourist information centre). Walk along New Bridge Street, cross South Harbour Street and cross the bridge over the River Ayr, where there are good views towards the Auld Brig on the right.

AULD BRIG AND NEW BRIDGE

The River Ayr has been crossed by various means for centuries, initially by just a ford. By the 13th century a timber bridge was being used to cross to the opposite bank. This was rebuilt in stone in around 1470. It is a beautiful, distinctive piece of architecture that survives to the present day. A 'New' Bridge was built in 1788 (hence the older bridge is known as Auld Brig) but it washed away during flooding in around 1870. It was replaced in 1878 by the equally distinctive bridge we cross today.

Once over the bridge cross North Harbour Street and continue into Main Street, which passes a variety of shops, pubs and restaurants. Cross Crown Street and continue to a waymarked signpost. Here bear left into Peebles Street. Walk along this street away from Ayr to its end. Turn left onto Waggon Road and then right onto

Glebe Road. Walk along the pavement towards the large gasworks building, crossing Glebe Crescent and Elmbank Street to climb towards Limekiln Road.

Looking back to the New Bridge and the magnificent spire of Ayr Town Hall

At Limekiln Road turn left and walk over a railway bridge onto Weir Road. Carefully descend the road (there is no pavement) as it sweeps round to the right towards an industrial estate and then turns left onto Saltpans Road. Walk to the road end and then turn right onto Newton's esplanade above **Woodfield**. Continue on past some factories, with the shore below the sea wall to the left and great views of Troon ahead. Walk along the esplanade, passing a car park to reach its end, cross Bellrock Road and continue onto a rough track. This climbs up onto a sandy track that continues above the shore and alongside the perimeter fence beside **Prestwick St Nicholas golf course**. The great houses of Prestwick can be seen across from the golf course.

Prestwick translates from Old English *Preost Wic* as Priest's Town as it was formerly an outlying religious

73

house. It became a burgh in 1170 and held regular markets thereafter. The town is probably best known for the fact that its golf course held the first ever Open Championship in 1860 (played over 12 holes compared to today's standard of 18). Old Tom Morris, the first great golf course designer and winner of the Open four times, designed the course in 1851 and it held the first 12 consecutive Open Championships. It went on to hold the competition 24 times in total, the last in 1925. Although the course is still a great test, even for the best golfers, the town does not have the amenities to be able to accommodate the vast crowds that attend today's Open Championships.

Elvis Presley famously landed at the airport in 1960 on his way home after military service in Germany. It was a fleeting visit of just one hour and remains his only documented visit to the UK.

Walk along the track towards Bentfield and, at the end of the golf course perimeter fence, bear left at a waymarked signpost down onto a gravelly track. At the bottom of the track turn right onto the stony beach and head towards Prestwick. You can see a number of jumbo jets leave and enter Prestwick Airport. ◀ The stony beach continues past a line of large sea defences and a few houses at **Bentfield**. Continue round the point towards the impressive seafront of **Prestwick**, which lies ahead. At Prestwick promenade come off the beach and walk along the promenade, passing Prestwick Sailing Club and the big red sandstone houses that line the seafront.

If the tide is too high then cut right up onto the dunes and walk along the path but, because of erosion, it is recommended that you stay off the dunes unless absolutely necessary.

At the far end of the promenade pass a car park and a children's play park to reach the circular red brick building for Scottish Water. Bear left here onto the fantastic broad sandy beach. ◀ Walk along the beach alongside the dunes and the famous **Prestwick golf course**. The beach is very pleasant underfoot after having had to walk along pavements for so long.

About 500m on from the water tower a green waymarked sign at the dunes indicates the point to come off the beach. A detour is required to enable walkers to use bridges to cross the river. Turn right off the beach and follow a distinct path through the dunes, which leads onto the north end of the golf course.

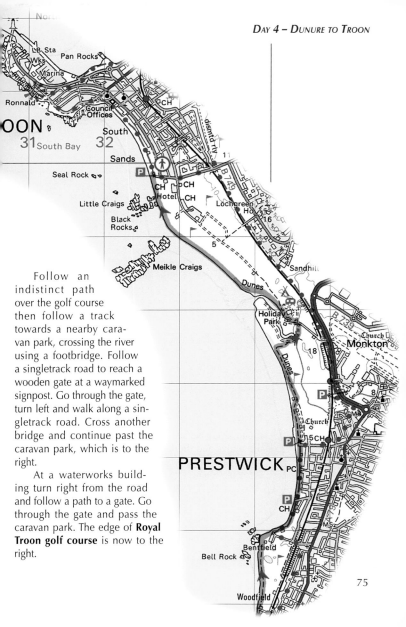

Follow an indistinct path over the golf course then follow a track towards a nearby caravan park, crossing the river using a footbridge. Follow a singletrack road to reach a wooden gate at a waymarked signpost. Go through the gate, turn left and walk along a singletrack road. Cross another bridge and continue past the caravan park, which is to the right.

At a waterworks building turn right from the road and follow a path to a gate. Go through the gate and pass the caravan park. The edge of **Royal Troon golf course** is now to the right.

75

Formed in 1878, **Royal Troon** is yet another of the many magnificent golf courses on the Ayrshire coast. Its Old Course is one of the host courses of the Open Championship and has hosted the competition eight times, the first in 1923. Royal Troon's Par 3 8th (better known as The Postage Stamp) is one of the most famous holes in golf.

Turn left here and follow a narrow path alongside the river through gorse bushes towards the coast. The path climbs over the dunes and then descends back down onto the beach at the southern end of **Troon**.

Translating from the Gaelic *An t-sron* simply as The Headland, **Troon**'s initial development was around its harbour. The town really began to expand in 1808 when William Bentinck, the 4th Duke of Portland, added docks. By the 1800s Troon had established itself as one of Britain's premier coal ports and a ship-yard was opened in 1860. Small-scale shipbuilding only ceased in 2000. Today a catamaran service runs

Last light at Troon

between Troon and Larne in Northern Ireland and, like neighbouring Ayr, Troon is an extremely popular destination for tourists.

Firm sand alongside lofty dunes and tremendous views towards Arran mean this is another fantastic beach to walk along. Continue on the long stretch of sand, passing the golf course and the large sandstone villas on Troon's seafront. After passing the dunes, there are several points to turn right off the beach and onto the South Sands esplanade.

The awesome profile of Arran as seen from Troon, its jagged outline cast into silhouette by the setting sun

DAY 5
Troon to Ardrossan

Start	Troon South Sands esplanade NS 328 298
Finish	Ardrossan Ferry Terminal NS 224 422
Distance	Main route: 17 miles (27 km); alternative via Dundonald Castle: 27 miles (43km)
Time	Main route: 6 hours; alternative: 9½ hours
Maps	OS Landranger 70; OS Explorer 326 333 and 341
Terrain	Although a lot of miles are covered in this section, the walking is flat with great expanses of beach. Pavements, paths, cycle tracks and singletrack roads make the going relatively easy.
Refreshments	There are several shops, restaurants and pubs in Troon, Irvine, Kilwinning, Stevenston, Saltcoats and Ardrossan.
Public Transport	Troon railway station (services including Ayr, Kilmarnock and Glasgow) is on Barassie Street. Barassie, Irvine, Kilwinning, Stevenston, Saltcoats and Ardrossan all have their own stations. The train from Ardrossan Harbour station runs to Glasgow Central but if you wish to travel to Ayr then a change of trains is required at Kilwinning. Stagecoach buses operate services between Ardrossan and Irvine and between Irvine and Troon (see Appendix C for details).

The six miles between Troon and Irvine are predominantly along the beach, which is great for tired legs and sore feet. Away from the beach the walk continues past Irvine harbour and the Scottish Maritime Museum, then heads away from the coast through peaceful mixed woodland following riverside paths. The route includes a highly recommended short diversion into Kilwinning (the town's Abbey is especially worth visiting). The six final miles to Ardrossan lead back to the coast and further stretches of fantastic beach walking, passing the towns of Stevenston and Saltcoats to end with a final stroll round the promenade into Ardrossan.

Walk along the esplanade at **South Sands** round the sea wall with the beach below, passing Portland Terrace to join Titchfield Road. Walk along the pavement and pass a car park, after which the esplanade gives way to a pavement running alongside Titchfield Road and the shore. Follow the pavement to reach a huge grassy embankment. Turn left here and climb the path onto the top of the embankment, where there is a superb view of Arran. Walk along the embankment high above the shore to its end. Here the embankment descends down to a small car park opposite a sawmill. Walk past the sawmill and turn right at a waymarked sign, passing a row of cottages. Turn right onto Harbour Road, cross to the left-hand side and walk along the pavement to pass Port of Troon beside the harbour.

ALTERNATIVE

At this point you have the choice to take a diversion to the village of **Dundonald**, which is home to the historic **Dundonald Castle**. It is a long diversion that adds a further 10 miles (16km) and 3½ hours to the day. It leads well away from the coast and much of it is beside busy roads but the castle is of great interest and is well worth a visit. As you walk along Harbour Road turn right onto Bennadrove Road and then left onto Templehill. Walk along the pavement and turn left onto Portland Street, then cross Jubilee Road and Barassie Street to bear right onto Dundonald Road (A759). Proceed along the road away from Troon for 1½ miles to eventually reach the small village of **Loans**. Turn left onto Main Street and continue through Loans for 1 mile until you reach a minor road signposted The Smugglers Trail. Cross the A78 and follow the road, passing **Collennan Farm**. Continue onto a track that runs for approximately 2 miles. It passes Troon Reservoir before leading through woodland and countryside to reach Dundonald and Dundonald Castle.

Dundonald Castle sits above the small, attractive village of Dundonald, which lies a few miles inland from Troon. It is thought that the site where the castle stands has been occupied since around 2000BC, and a hill fort was built here between 500BC and 200BC. Although dating from the early 13th century Dundonald Castle itself was rebuilt in around 1370 for Robert II, who became King of Scotland in 1371 and died at the castle in 1390. Further additions were made to the building during the 15th century and it is thought that Dundonald Castle was inhabited into the 17th century. Although it is now a ruin, the castle is protected by Historic Scotland as an ancient monument and is a popular visitor attraction.

To continue to Irvine, retrace your steps back to The Smugglers Trail signpost and then turn right onto the A759. Follow the road to reach a roundabout. The route rejoins the NCN7 cycle track here, passing underneath the A78 and then along the edge of Shewalton Moss, a nature reserve that is home to kestrels and buzzards. A footpath then re-crosses the A78 before the cycle path skirts Gailes golf course for a further 2½ miles to reach **Irvine beach** underneath its prominent dragon monument. To continue, see page 83.

After a roundabout at a waymarked sign, turn left away from Harbour Road and climb a grassy embankment onto a path that continues onto **Barassie Sands**.

map continues on page 85

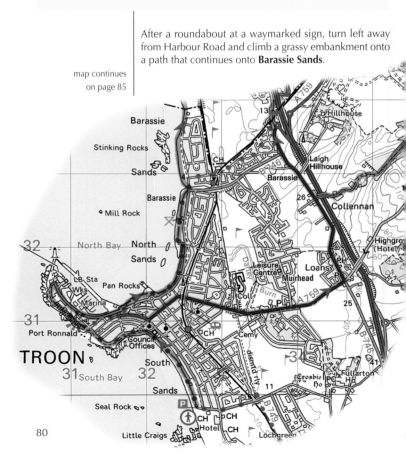

Barassie is a continuation of Troon that was originally founded as a holiday resort in 1830 bearing the name New Kilmarnock. The resort was slow to develop and eventually changed its name, taking Barassie from a local farm. The former name lives on today at Kilmarnock (Barassie) golf course.

▶ At Beach Road turn left to head down to the beach. It is a wonderful six miles of beach walking all the way to Irvine, the firm sand underfoot making for great walking. Arran's celebrated profile is part of the exceptional view throughout this section, allowing the mind to wander towards the next few days spent walking the island's beautiful coastline.

To the right of the beach runs Beach Road with its line of sandstone houses. After passing the houses follow a path over an outflow pipe and walk towards the dunes. The burn here can be tricky

If the tide is too high stay off the beach and continue along Harbour Road. Proceed straight through two roundabouts onto North Shore Road.

Dundonald Castle lies a few miles inland from Barassie

Arran from Barassie in winter

to cross after periods of heavy rainfall and around high tide. ▸ After crossing it walk back onto the beach to continue towards Irvine. The houses have now been replaced by some great sand dunes and **Kilmarnock (Barassie) golf course** to the right.

There are a few similar burns that require crossing by the same method as you progress along the beach.

Continue along the beach past the sand dunes, which rise to around 15ft in height. **Western Gailes golf course** is now beyond them to the right. As Irvine is approached a conspicuous dragon sculpture above the beach comes into view. Here there is a choice of routes. The first is to simply continue to walk the final mile along the beach to **Irvine Beach Park**, leaving the sand at the point indicated below. The second is to turn right off the beach onto a path through the dunes marked by a tall wooden post and to follow it to reach a waymarked sign.

▸ If you have taken the alternative route to Dundonald Castle, rejoin the main route here. Irvine is now to the right.

Turn left onto a faint path and climb to the dragon sculpture. There are great views from this position along the coast and out towards Arran. From here continue down the path alongside attractive parkland beside the dunes, with some industrial buildings and **Irvine** to the right.

The path follows the line of dunes and then passes a man-made lochan to the right to reach the **Beach Park** car park and public toilets. Turn left and walk round the toilets along the pavement.

▸ If you have continued along the sand, leave it here.

Walk through the car park, passing the Automatic Tide Marker Station to head towards Irvine's harbour. Pass the Bridge of Scottish Invention (a retractable footbridge built in 2000) and join Harbour Street.

Irvine's harbour and the River Irvine at dusk

The unique **Automatic Tide Marker Station**, designed in 1905 by Irvine's harbourmaster Martin Boyd, stands at the confluence of the Rivers Garnock and Irvine. When in regular use, this square building had a pole on top with 12 large balls attached to it. As the tide came in and out the balls would move up and down, allowing sailors to gauge the depth of the water at the mouth of the river.

IRVINE

The origins of Irvine go way back to the Romans, with the town standing on or near the Roman centre of Vindogara, which existed between the first and third centuries. It achieved burgh status in 1140 and royal burgh status in 1371. Irvine is classed as one of Scotland's 'New Towns' after major redevelopment in the 1960s. New towns featuring modern architecture and business parks were created to cope with the overspill of an ever-burgeoning Glasgow population. However, the designs of the new buildings were not always popular with residents as they sat incongruously against the more traditional aspects of the old town. The harbour, which is built alongside the River Irvine, has several interesting buildings including The Ship Inn, which opened for business in 1754. The Scottish Maritime Museum also sits near the harbour. Irvine's harbour was once one of Glasgow's main trading ports and the museum exhibits Scotland's fantastic heritage with the sea.

map continues
on page 89

A fishing trawler, sitting off the coast at Irvine, bears the brunt of a freezing winter dawn

Walk along the pavement, passing a selection of working and leisure boats moored in the River Irvine. The **Magnum Centre**, Harbour Arts Centre and a selection of cafés, pubs and restaurants line Harbour Street. It is a fine setting to stop for a drink or a bite to eat. It is here that the Ayrshire Coastal Path journeys away from the coast due to the River Irvine and the nature of the surrounding terrain. Continue along Harbour Street towards the town centre, passing part of the **Scottish Maritime Museum** to the left. The museum's main entrance is on the right at the end of Linthouse Vennel.

Harbour Street continues onto Montgomery Street. The road then sweeps round to the left (opposite Irvine Railway Station) into Cochrane Street, which ends at the Victoria roundabout. Cross the road and follow the roundabout to the right into Church Street, passing a waymarked sign. Follow Church Street underneath the railway bridge to Marress roundabout, with Fullarton Church on the left and Cunninghame House and Rivergate shopping centre on the right. The road then turns left onto Double Dykes Road (the A737) towards Kilwinning.

Walk away from Irvine town centre with the A737 road to the right and the railway to the left. Follow the pavement as it sweeps round to the right, taking you through the A737 underpass onto the signed No. 7 cycle track and into a small estate. A waymarked sign 50m further on directs you across a side street and onto a metal bridge that crosses the River Irvine.

After crossing the bridge turn left onto a path. Walk under the A737 along the riverbank where there is a variety of wildlife to enjoy including herons, moorhens and kingfishers. The path then climbs above the river, passing a housing estate. ▶

Arran and the coast come back into view here.

The path then splits at a statue of Robert Burns (erected in 1896 on the centenary of Burns' death). Take the left-hand path (signed Cycle Path 7) and walk alongside the open grassland to reach a wall beside the railway track. The path sweeps round to the right and, after 200m, veers away from the railway line to reach a waymarked sign at a minor road. Cross the road and take the right-hand path (the path to the left leads towards the site of the former Bogside railway station) and walk along the flat path through pleasant mixed woodland. Although the views are limited here this section of the route is away from any main roads, so it is very peaceful. Buzzards, squirrels and (if you're very fortunate) roe deer are in close proximity.

The path continues to Bartonholm Recycling Centre at Sandy Road. Turn left onto Sandy Road and follow the pavement, passing Garnock Floods Wildlife Reserve to reach a waymarked sign at a road bridge. Walk across the bridge over the **River Garnock**, then turn right off Sandy Road onto a good, broad track through mixed woodland. Continue on the track as it sweeps to the left and passes under the A78 via an underpass.

The track then leads away from the A78 towards Eglinton Country Park, through more mixed woodland along the riverbank to a junction of paths. Take the left-hand path (the right leads into the country park). From here, it is ¾ of a mile to Kilwinning and 6 miles to Ardrossan. Follow the track for 100m to another junction

The impressive Kilwinning Abbey was founded between 1140 and 1191

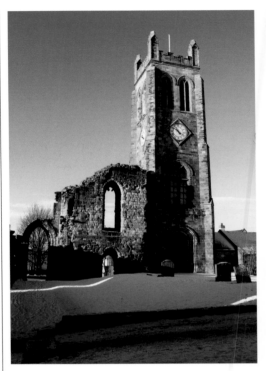

and a signpost indicating Ardrossan straight on. Ignore this for the time being and turn right to walk along the track by the River Garnock into **Kilwinning**.

Kilwinning is named after Saint Winnin, who settled here in AD715. The town is notable for being the home of the original Masonic Lodge, which is thought to date from 1150. It still holds Lodge Number 0 and is known as the Mother Lodge of Scotland. Due to the many rail links that pass through Kilwinning the town is known as the Crossroads of Ayrshire.

As you approach the town the path climbs a flight of steps. At the top turn right onto Dovecot Lane and walk towards the town centre. Turn left to cross Church Street and continue onto Main Street. There is a good choice of shops, restaurants and pubs here for provisions and refreshments. Continue along Main Street to a pub called The Lemon Tree and then turn left into **Kilwinning Abbey**.

The marvellous **Kilwinning Abbey** was established between 1140 and 1191 after several centuries of Christian worship in the area. It was built for Tironensian Benedictine Monks by Hugh de Morville, a Norman knight who also founded Dryburgh Abbey. For the next few centuries Kilwinning Abbey was a magnificent, affluent monastery but its downfall began in the 16th century and its last abbot, Gavin Hamilton, was killed at Restalrig near Edinburgh in 1571. Over the next 30 years the abbey was dismantled and its stone used for other nearby buildings including a new parish church. The original south transept, however, still stands today. In 1815 the 103ft clock tower was built at a cost of £2000.

map continues
on page 90

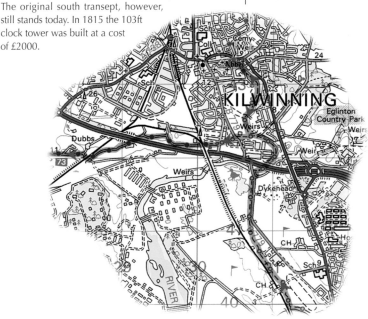

Retrace your steps back to the signpost for Ardrossan at the riverbank track and turn right. Walk through an industrial estate for 100m and then cross the road at a waymarked sign. Walk along the path, which leaves the adjacent road to pass through a short section of woodland, to regain the road at a large Core Path signpost for Dubbs Road. The singletrack road (also Cycle Track 73) runs parallel to the A78 on the left and continues alongside a corrugated iron fence. Walk under the railway line and continue along the singletrack road by a line of trees to the left and open grassland to the right for pleasant, peaceful walking. The road passes underneath the A78 and then past Todhill Country Centre.

Walk along the road beside Todhill Community Woodland, pass under the railway again and continue as the road turns to the left and passes a variety of farm buildings. Continue to walk along Dubbs Road, passing Broom Farm and then Greenacres Caravan Park to reach the end of Dubbs Road at the junction with the B752. Carefully cross the main road to reach a lovely woodland path on the opposite side, which leads away from the B752.

The path then opens out into parkland with views of the town of Stevenston to your right. Keep to the left of the parkland and follow the path to a waymarked sign that points straight on. After 100m the path

map continues on page 93

sweeps to the right through the parkland. After passing the pond to the right the path continues onto Moorpark Road East and into **Stevenston**.

Saltcoats and Arran seen beyond the snow left by freezing temperatures on Stevenston beach

> **Stevenston** is the most easterly of Ayrshire's Three Towns, a name used to describe Stevenston, Saltcoats and Ardrossan together. They merge almost imperceptibly together as you walk along the coast and to the visitor may appear to be one place, but the three towns retain their separate community identities to locals. Stevenston was established in the 12th century but, surprisingly, did not receive burgh status until 1952 and so is the newest burgh in Ayrshire. Coal, rather than fishing, was its main industry from the 17th century until local pits were exhausted near the end of the 19th century.

Walk along Moorpark Road East then turn left onto Station Road. A pavement continues along Station Road through Stevenston (with a good variety of shops) and crosses Portland Place. Cross the railway track at Stevenston Railway Station then cross Warner Street to lead onto Shore Road.

At Ardeer Church cross Caledonian Road and continue to walk along Shore Road. As the road splits take the right-hand fork and walk towards the beach, passing open parkland and football pitches to the left and right. Continue along the pavement to the road end and turn right into a car park. Follow the road through the car park to a waymarked sign at a metal bridge, which crosses a river and leads onto Stevenston beach.

Turn right onto the beach, which provides great walking after the last few miles of tarmac as well as fantastic views of Saltcoats and out towards Arran. Follow the beach to a large sea wall, climb the short slope onto a pavement beside the railway track and walk along the pavement. Continue right round the sea front into the town of **Saltcoats**.

> **Saltcoats** is the second of Ayrshire's Three Towns and, not surprisingly, salt has played a major role in the town's development. The name derives from the cots (or cottages) that were once home to salt workers, who created rock salt by evaporating seawater in the town's saltpans. However, at the turn of the 20th century a finer grade of salt began to be imported from Liverpool and the industry in Saltcoats was unable to survive. Coal mining and fishing were also prominent early industries while in the 1960s and 70s Saltcoats, thanks to its sandy beaches and outdoor swimming pool, became a major destination for day-trippers and holidaymakers during Glasgow's Fair Fortnight, which, at the time, was the principal two-week summer holiday for Glaswegians in July.

At a waymarked sign walk straight on, passing some flats to reach another waymarked sign. It is attached to the sea wall and points right, directing you onto the promenade at the southern end of **Ardrossan**.

Walk along the promenade towards Ardrossan's South Bay. Continue round the sea wall, passing a play park and an outdoor swimming pool (a reminder of a time when Saltcoats and Ardrossan were popular holiday destinations) towards the great sandstone houses lining the sea front.

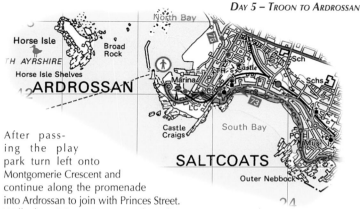

After passing the play park turn left onto Montgomerie Crescent and continue along the promenade into Ardrossan to join with Princes Street. Walk along Princes Street over the railway crossing then turn left into Harbour Road. Walk down Harbour Road, cross a roundabout beside a supermarket and then go over another railway crossing to continue along the pavement towards the Caledonian MacBrayne ferry terminal. The joys of the next four days on Arran await.

Ardrossan is now indelibly linked with Arran due to the regular daily ferry service between the two but the town has a rich history all of its own; its roots stretch back as far as 1140 when Ardrossan Castle was built on Castle Hill (known locally as Cannon Hill). In 1292 the castle fell into English hands and was held until 1296 when one William Wallace, the famous patriot and freedom fighter, tricked the English garrison by setting a decoy fire in the town. When the soldiers left the castle to investigate, Wallace butchered them and tossed their remains in the dungeon, which has since been known as Wallace's Larder. In the mid-16th century the castle fell into Oliver Cromwell's hands, which he then destroyed to use much of the stonework to build his fort at Ayr. Coal and fishing helped in Ardrossan's development. Passenger services between Ardrossan and Brodick began in 1834 and the route is now synonymous with the iconic, red-funnelled, Caledonian MacBrayne ferries.

DAY 6

Brodick to Lochranza

Start	Brodick Ferry Terminal NS 022 359
Finish	Lochranza Castle NR 933 507
Distance	16 miles (26 km)
Time	7 hours
Maps	OS Landranger 69; OS Explorer 361
Terrain	This is a tough section that uses pavements, beach, rough cycle track and woodland paths. It also features some remote sections of shoreline path where boulder hopping is necessary. Some of the terrain is awkward to cross, which can slow progress and make for quite a long day.
Refreshments	Brodick has a vast array of shops, pubs and restaurants; Corrie has a more limited selection; Lochranza has hotels but no shop.
Public Transport	There is an excellent bus service that runs between Lochranza and Brodick, the times of which coincide with the Brodick to Ardrossan ferry. See Appendix C for details.

The 16 miles from Brodick to Lochranza feature extremely diverse terrain and breathtaking scenery throughout. From the ferry terminal a pavement leads through the bustling town of Brodick and round beautiful Brodick Bay, where there are fantastic views towards the island's iconic mountains. Away from the town a quiet section of rough cycle track climbs high above the coast and down into Corrie, where there are some amazing rocks and boulders along the shoreline. Once through Corrie and on past Sannox the next few miles to Lochranza are along very remote coastal paths, well away from any roads or human habitation – peace and quiet guaranteed. The exceptional wildlife to see on this stretch includes seals, sea otters and, if you are very lucky, dolphins. The going can be awkward at times when boulder-strewn beaches are encountered, especially at the An Scriodan rock fall. This does not cause too many problems at lower tides but, when they are higher, progress can be tricky over the steep, rough ground. The final section to Lochranza passes Newton's Point, where the renowned Scottish geologist James Hutton found several geological formations to use as evidence for his theories regarding the formation of the earth.

From **Brodick** Ferry Terminal walk past the Caledonian MacBrayne ticket office and cross the entrance to the bus terminal. The pavement then crosses a bridge over a small harbour and continues along the promenade through Brodick and alongside the beach. Walk along the promenade until you reach a putting green.

The iconic red-funnelled ferries of **Caledonian MacBrayne** ply their trade between most of the west coast Scottish islands and the mainland and they have become an integral part of island life and tourism. The sailing from Oban to South Uist is the longest the company offers and takes over five hours while the shortest, Colintraive on the Cowal Peninsula to Bute, lasts only five minutes. Established in 1851 as David Hutcheson & Co., the company became Caledonian MacBrayne in 1870 when Hutcheson retired, handing over full control to one of its partners, David MacBrayne, who subsequently changed the name. The company has gone through various guises over the years. Today it is publicly owned and controlled by the Scottish Government.

map continues on page 99

Pass the putting green and turn right to walk down a side road through a car park, continuing onto a path that passes a children's swing park and then crosses a wooden bridge. Once across the bridge bear right and walk along a good path that remains above the beach, skirting the perimeter of **Brodick golf course**. Cross another footbridge and continue along the path beside a fairway to reach a large iron bridge that crosses the lovely Glenrosa Water. Walk across the bridge, turn right

Brodick's lovely sweeping bay provides a superb panorama of the island's mountains

and follow the path alongside the river as it bears left and continues through some gorse bushes. Walk along the path as it keeps to the edge of the golf course and eventually leads to a third bridge. Cross here then walk a short section of path into a car park, passing the buildings of the Arran Mountain Rescue Centre.

BRODICK

The name Brodick derives from the Old Norse *Breithr Vik*, meaning Broad Bay. Its Gaelic name, *Traigh Chasteal*, means Shore of the Castle, and harks back to when the main landing port and village was situated across the bay where Brodick Castle stands today. Although not the largest settlement on the island (which is actually Lamlash) the fact that the ferry docks here means Brodick is a busy place with many shops, restaurants and cafés lining the front. The town also has a marvellous outlook with the fantastic, jagged profiles of Goat Fell, Cir Mhòr, Caisteal Abhail and Beinn Tarsuinn rising steeply across the bay.

At the exit of the car park, opposite **Cladach**, turn right onto the A841. At this point the road does not have any pavement so take care when walking along the grass verge (although the road is not overly busy). Continue away from Brodick, passing the entrance to Shore Lodge to reach the entrance of **Brodick Castle and Country Park**.

BRODICK CASTLE

It is very much worthwhile to take the short walk up the drive to reach Brodick Castle and its wonderful gardens. It is thought that the site has been used as a defended fort since the time of Arran's Viking occupation in the 11th century and the castle has had a very turbulent history since. It has passed through many hands over the centuries, including being occupied by English forces during the Wars of Scottish Independence in the late 13th and early 14th centuries. Now owned by the National Trust for Scotland, the beauty of the castle's external facade is equalled by its sumptuous interior.

Brodick Castle and gardens

Past the castle entrance the grass verge gives way to a low sea wall above the northern end of Brodick beach. Continue to walk along the roadside to the entrance of **Merkland Wood**. Carefully cross the road here and walk into Merkland Wood onto a broad track that climbs steadily away from the main road.

After crossing a bridge the track climbs a little more steeply to reach a fork. Here continue straight on. The track then begins to zigzag its way through the forest to reach another fork, which is waymarked for Corrie. At this point turn right and continue to climb the track, passing a clearing in the forest with the rounded slopes of **Maol Donn** rising to the left. The track then becomes stonier as it gradually ascends and descends through the forest, with only a few brief, but magnificent, views across to the Ayrshire mainland. ◄

The track begins to descend quite steeply back down towards the A841, turning sharply to the right then left down to a gate. Go through the gate and follow the path for a short distance to the main road. Cross the road, turn left and walk along the roadside into the village of **Corrie**, which is a long, attractive village with a series of lovely cottages lining its seafront.

During spring and summer there are a fine variety of wildflowers along the way in this section including wood anemone and red campion.

Stunning erratic boulders on the shore near Corrie

THE GEOLOGY OF CORRIE

The stretch of coastline beside the village of Corrie and stretching further north to Sannox features a remarkable selection of wonderfully erratic boulders. They rest on the beaches here after having been carried down from the mountains by glaciers around 15,000 years ago. Contrasting with the boulders are the long, sinuous lines of red sandstone, which have contorted into a series of incredible shapes over the millennia.

Walk along the road above the shore, passing a small **harbour**, and continue through the village. Pass a **hotel**, cross a bridge (where the road is quite narrow) and pass another harbour.

map continues on page 101

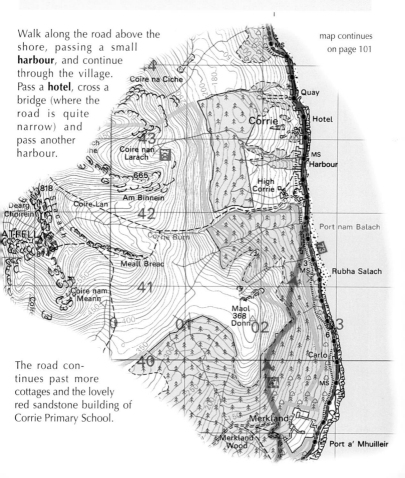

The road continues past more cottages and the lovely red sandstone building of Corrie Primary School.

The A841 continues out of Corrie and on towards Sannox. Again there is no pavement here so keep a careful eye out for traffic in both directions. Buses and lorries use the road so keep to the side as much as possible. En route the huge Clach na Chath (Stone of Battle) is passed, which a soldier of Oliver Cromwell's is said to have hid behind during a bloody battle in which Cromwell's men successfully captured Brodick Castle in 1652.

In **Sannox** continue through the village, passing a pier and a line of fine cottages. Like many of the place names on Arran, Sannox derives from Old Norse: in this case from *Sandr Vik*, meaning Sand Bay. At the end of Sannox walk past a small cark park on the right-hand side of the A841. Turn right off the road and walk the short distance down to a river and cross it by means of some large concrete blocks. ◀

These are simple to cross but if you would rather not there is a road bridge that crosses the river a short distance further along the main road.

On the opposite side of the river walk away from it and turn right onto a path, which passes through gorse and heads towards the beach. Turn left and continue through more gorse, passing several houses and a navigation beacon. The steep, rocky slopes of **Goat Fell** and Caisteal Abhail rise sharply from here and provide a really dramatic backdrop to the walk. Continue by some steep cliffs rising to the left into a section of woodland.

Horses cross the North Sannox Burn

Walk through the woods along a good path that veers to the left away from the shore to run parallel with the North Sannox Burn, which has a series of lovely waterfalls. (Alternatively, cross the burn

map continues
on page 103

here via the stepping stones, which saves the next 1km.) At a bridge, turn right from the path to cross the burn, then turn right and walk along a single-track road through more woodland leading to a car park at a picnic site. Walk through the car park to reach a gate. Go through it and walk through a lovely section of mixed woodland that is home to a vast array of plants and animals including bluebells and red squirrels. A broad track continues through the woodland and then past a substantial forest plantation.

At the edge of the forest the track merges with a sandy path and here a deer fence to the left follows the line of the path to reach a gate. Go through the gate (the fence is now to the right) and walk along the track. When it

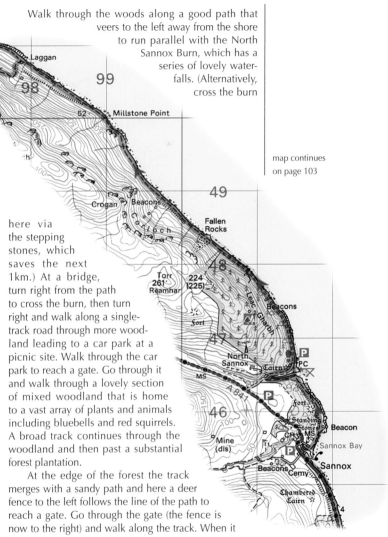

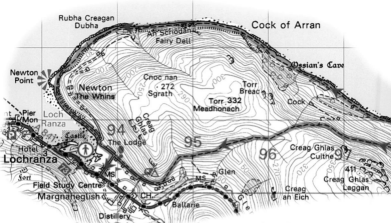

splits take the left-hand fork, which makes its way along the coast.

Make your way past some huge boulders on the beach and then pass underneath another large navigation beacon that sits high up on the steep ground rising to the left. Walk along the shore on the excellent path, which continues past **Millstone Point** and offers superb views along this rugged and secluded stretch of coastline. The path gives excellent walking on this section and, above, many waterfalls tumble down the steep slopes of **Creag Ghlas Laggan**.

*The remote
Laggan Cottage*

The path then passes the extensive remains of sheep pens and crosses a burn by means of a wooden footbridge, continuing on to reach the very remote **Laggan Cottage**. Those who lived here in the past must have enjoyed their own company as it is very isolated, well away from any towns, villages and roads with only a couple of paths in and out. One such path climbs west away from the cottage to reach Lochranza and is an alternative route in case of high tide.

Along with the ruin of Cock Farm further inland, **Laggan** is a remnant of a formerly thriving community in this area, which included a family called MacMillan. Daniel MacMillan (1813–1857) was born on Arran and went on, with his brother Alexander, to found the renowned MacMillan publishing company in London. In 1957 his grandson Harold became UK Prime Minister.

If the tide looks high when you reach Laggan Cottage it will in all likelihood be too high to cross the **An Scriodan** rock fall further along the main coastal route. If this is the case, take the path west away from the cottage to head inland.

ALTERNATIVE FINISH

The steep path climbs over some wild and remote country and is a taxing route. Fitness levels, as well as navigational skills, would have to be considered if thinking of using it. To follow it, bear left just before **Laggan Cottage** onto an excellent path that zigzags its way up grassy slopes below the crags of **Creag Ghlas Cuithe**. As the ruin of **Cock Farm** comes into view to the right the path climbs steeply to reach a broad plateau underneath **Torr Meadhonach** and a cairn at 263m where there are excellent views in all directions. The path then continues in a westerly direction beside the Allt Chailean and above Glen Chalmadale, with good views of the distillery at Lochranza. It now begins to descend towards the village, eventually reaching a singletrack road. Turn right here to walk along the road and pass **Lochranza golf course**, then turn left onto another singletrack road and follow it to reach the A841. Turn right and continue to the route's finish at **Lochranza Castle**.

The Cock of Arran, the island's most northerly point

Keeping to the shore, walk past Laggan Cottage along a firm, grassy path. As a wooded glen is approached the path forks. Take the left-hand fork to climb gradually into the wood, passing a huge boulder on the way. The wood consists of some wonderfully gnarled trees. Upon reaching a waymarked signpost at the top of the slope turn right to descend a muddy path and then turn left onto some rockier ground. Walk along the path, passing some crumbling, stone buildings: a stark reminder that this area was once home to a thriving salt business during the 18th century known as Duchess Anne's Salt Pans.

After passing the buildings continue beside the shore and pass a large wood to the left. The path then continues over rockier ground, passing a couple of smaller woods. It then leads through an opening in a wall, underneath the wooded slopes of Leacann Dubh. As you approach the huge, shapely boulder of the **Cock of Arran** (which marks the northerly tip of the island) the path becomes extremely boggy due to the flatter ground along the shore catching all the water that runs off the surrounding hills. There is a remarkable range of geology along this whole section, from small perfectly formed pebbles to wonderful slabs of sandstone. The views across the Sound of Bute towards the Cumbraes and to Bute are superb.

From the Cock of Arran continue underneath the cliffs of **Torr Meadhonach** towards the **An Scriodan** rock fall, which is a section of boulders that can cause route-finding problems at higher tide. ▸ If the tide is high on arrival then the steep, awkward ground above the shore will have to be traversed, considerably slowing your progress. At lower tides walk along the path as it gradually climbs away from the shore through the initial section of An Scriodan.

As it progresses the path becomes less distinct and it is then a matter of carefully scrambling over the rocks and boulders to reach the shore. Walk along the stony beach, which comprises beautifully smooth coloured pebbles, to then pick up a grassy track leading to **Fairy Dell**.

Walk past the cottage at Fairy Dell, cross a burn and continue along the coastline by **Rubha Creagan Dubha**, with steep slopes rising to the left. The path is a mixture of good, firm walking although at certain points it can be extremely boggy. Continue along the path to reach a waymarked post and then bear right onto an indistinct

Check the tide times before setting out along this section.

The remains of Lochranza Castle

105

grassy track that heads back towards the shore, reaching another waymarked post. Turn left here onto a very peaceful section of the route, with good views towards Kintyre. Continue underneath an embankment along a raised beach. The ground is still boggy but eventually the path improves as it approaches Newton Point. The path passes **Newton Point** and, as you continue towards **Loch Ranza**, the view towards the jagged profile of Caisteal Abhail is incredible.

> In 1787 James Hutton, the renowned Scottish geologist known as the father of modern geology, found evidence at Newton Point to support his theory of unconformity and his hypothesis that Earth was much older than previously thought. In the following year his *Theory of the Earth* was published, in which he tried to explain the rock formations he had found throughout Scotland and how they related to the earth's formation.

The path then merges with a singletrack road at South Newton. Walk along the road, which passes several cottages beside Loch Ranza and offers good views to Lochranza Castle and to the village of **Lochranza** itself. Continue along the road and then turn right onto another singletrack road. Cross a bridge over a river and continue to the road end, then turn right onto the A841 and walk along the roadside to **Lochranza Castle**.

> Translating beautifully from the Gaelic *Loch Raonasa* as The Loch of the Rowan Tree River, Loch Ranza is a sea loch. Here, predominantly on its south side, sits the village of **Lochranza**, which used to be a major herring port. It is surrounded on three sides by high slopes and is home to the Isle of Arran Distillery as well as Lochranza Castle. The castle is now a ruin (although it is open to the public) but its history stretches back to the 1200s, when it was built for the MacSween Clan. From around 1380 it was used as a hunting seat for Scottish kings.

DAY 7
Lochranza to Blackwaterfoot

Start	Lochranza Castle NR 933 507
Finish	Car park at Blackwaterfoot NR 895 283
Distance	17 miles (27 km)
Time	7 hours
Maps	OS Landranger 69; OS Explorer 361
Terrain	This section runs down the length of Arran's quieter west coast and is this guide's longest route on the island. Much of it is along roadside verge beside the rocky shore but it is also interspersed with short sections of beach, hillside, woodland paths and forest tracks. Apart from the section between Lochranza and Catacol, the route's difficulty can be described as simple.
Refreshments	This route has long stretches between villages and there are only a couple en route. There are no shops in Lochranza, although there are hotels (see Appendix B). Pirnmill has a shop with a post office and a restaurant. Machrie has a tea room at the golf course (with limited opening hours). Blackwaterfoot has shops and a hotel.
Public Transport	There is an excellent bus service that runs between Lochranza and Blackwaterfoot. Several buses from the latter leave at times coinciding with the Brodick to Ardrossan ferry. See Appendix C for details.

Although much of the route between Lochranza and Blackwaterfoot is along roadside verge, the scenery of the walk is thoroughly inspiring. The crystal clear waters of the Kilbrannan Sound are almost constant as are the wonderful views towards the Kintyre Peninsula. A single diversion away from the coast to see the Machrie Standing Stones is well worth the effort. The day is book-ended by two fantastic sections of hillside path and dramatic shoreline. The Postman's Path climbs high above the Kilbrannan Sound from Lochranza, passing one of the oldest houses on Arran and continuing through some peaceful woodland that grants fantastic views and wildlife including chaffinches and meadow pipits. The final few miles to Blackwaterfoot use forest tracks (featuring possibly the best view available on the whole route) leading to King's Cave and onwards to the great cliffs of Drumadoon Point. The 12-hole Shiskine golf course (one of Scotland's finest) is passed before the path heads towards the white sands at Drumadoon Bay and into Blackwaterfoot.

From **Lochranza Castle** walk northwest along the A841 beside the waters of **Loch Ranza** towards the Caledonian MacBrayne ferry terminal. At a signpost for Claonaig Ferry turn left off the main road and climb the track that heads west away from Loch Ranza, passing several cottages as it heads towards Coillemore. The singletrack road climbs steadily and then joins a rough stony track that provides lovely views back towards Loch Ranza and Newton Point. The track meanders its way up the hillside, passing the last whitewashed cottage to meet **Coillemore**, which is one of the oldest houses on Arran. It is a ruin now but it is still very atmospheric and its position gives sumptuous views.

The remains of Coillemore above Lochranza, one of the oldest houses on Arran

The track stops here but there is an indistinct path that leads away to the right of Coillemore. This path, which runs down into Catacol, is known as the Postman's Path.

Turn left onto it and follow it along the hillside between a thick line of ferns. As you progress the path becomes clearer and it soon forks at a yellow marker post. Take the right-hand fork and continue. ▸ Pass a couple of further yellow marker posts to continue high above the shore.

This section of the path can be quite boggy at times.

The path can be overgrown as it leads through birch trees and rhododendron bushes but it becomes more obvious as it continues into woodland. There is plenty of wildlife in these woods including deer, stonechats, butterflies, crowberry and foxglove. Some of the trees are daubed with yellow paint, signifying that you are on the right track. If you look down to the right there are great views of the Lochranza to Claonaig ferry as well as across to Kintyre. The path continues between open hillside and further pockets of woodland, passing some wooden telegraph poles, crossing a narrow burn and then heading into an old birch wood. At times the path through the wood can be a bit stony. There are also tree roots underfoot as well as low, overhanging branches, so take care.

map continues on page 110

Cross another burn. The path then climbs steadily through some fairly thick undergrowth and heads through a longer stretch of woodland to cross a third burn. Eventually the path begins to descend steeply towards **Catacol** and it gives good views of Arran's quieter west coastline. Here you can take in the lovely beaches and undulating western hills including Meall nan Damh.

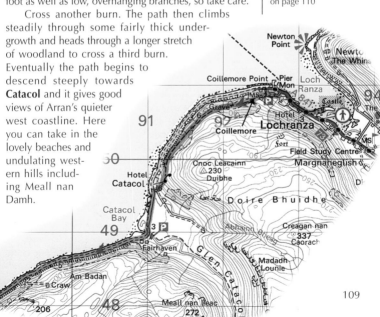

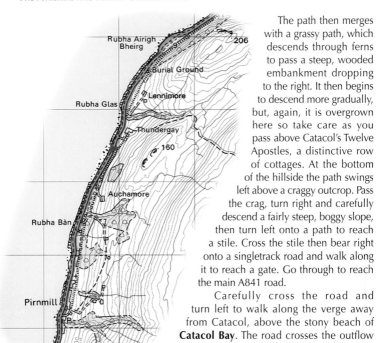

map continues
on page 112

The path then merges with a grassy path, which descends through ferns to pass a steep, wooded embankment dropping to the right. It then begins to descend more gradually, but, again, it is overgrown here so take care as you pass above Catacol's Twelve Apostles, a distinctive row of cottages. At the bottom of the hillside the path swings left above a craggy outcrop. Pass the crag, turn right and carefully descend a fairly steep, boggy slope, then turn left onto a path to reach a stile. Cross the stile then bear right onto a singletrack road and walk along it to reach a gate. Go through to reach the main A841 road.

Carefully cross the road and turn left to walk along the verge away from Catacol, above the stony beach of **Catacol Bay**. The road crosses the outflow of **Abhainn Bheag** and makes its way south-west, giving fine views of Arran's high western hills as well as across the crystal clear waters of the Kilbrannan Sound to Kintyre. It is best to stick to the road here due to the ruggedness of the shoreline, so the walking to Machrie is predominantly flat. The road itself is fairly quiet in terms of traffic due to there being no further major settlements until Blackwaterfoot.

Continue along the verge until the road crosses a lovely stone and metalled bridge at the outflow of Abhainn Mór at **Fairhaven**. From here the road continues away from Catacol Bay, passing underneath the steep, wooded slopes below **Meall nan Leac Sleamhuinn** and Meall nan Damh. The route then continues towards **Rubha Airigh Bheirg**, which features many fascinating rocks and boulders as well as birdlife including cormorants and red throated divers along its shoreline. It then passes through some steep-sided gorges where the road has been blasted through.

The road climbs quite high above the shore, allowing great views into the amazingly clear waters, before dropping back down. It continues beneath steep, wooded slopes to pass a very small burial ground at **Lennimore**. The graveyard sits right beside the main road and comprises around a dozen stones, the oldest dating from 1794.

After the graveyard the road passes through another gorge at **Rubha Glas**, which has some intriguing rocky outcrops. It then crosses a bridge over a burn and passes **Thundergay**, which comprises a few houses sitting high up on the hillside.

Walk along the roadside verge, passing a track to the left that leads to Coire Fhionn Lochan and continue alongside a low sea wall. ▸ Another road bridge is crossed to lead into the village of **Pirnmill**, which consists of a long line of cottages, a few B&Bs, a restaurant and a post office. As you pass through the village you will see the prominent Mullach Buidhe (the highest of Arran's western hills) as

There are some beautiful rounded stones on the beach here.

Looking towards Beinn Bharrain from Machrie Bay

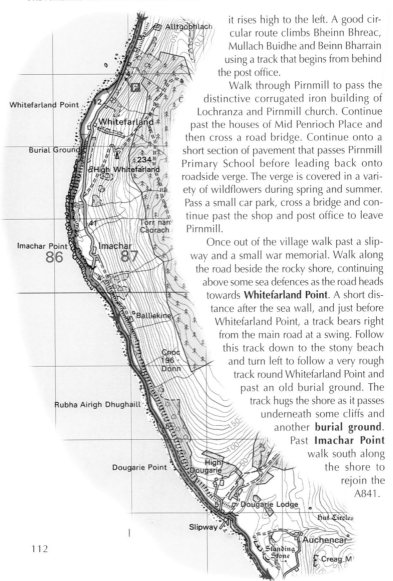

it rises high to the left. A good circular route climbs Bheinn Bhreac, Mullach Buidhe and Beinn Bharrain using a track that begins from behind the post office.

Walk through Pirnmill to pass the distinctive corrugated iron building of Lochranza and Pirnmill church. Continue past the houses of Mid Penrioch Place and then cross a road bridge. Continue onto a short section of pavement that passes Pirnmill Primary School before leading back onto roadside verge. The verge is covered in a variety of wildflowers during spring and summer. Pass a small car park, cross a bridge and continue past the shop and post office to leave Pirnmill.

Once out of the village walk past a slipway and a small war memorial. Walk along the road beside the rocky shore, continuing above some sea defences as the road heads towards **Whitefarland Point**. A short distance after the sea wall, and just before Whitefarland Point, a track bears right from the main road at a swing. Follow this track down to the stony beach and turn left to follow a very rough track round Whitefarland Point and past an old burial ground. The track hugs the shore as it passes underneath some cliffs and another **burial ground**. Past **Imachar Point** walk south along the shore to rejoin the A841.

It is now road walking all the way for about five miles, until the track for King's Cave past Machrie is reached. This is another quiet section of road that gives fine views south towards Drumadoon Point. There are many types of birdlife here including shags and oystercatchers.

Follow the A841 above the shore past **Rubha Airigh Dhughaill** and **Dougarie Point**. The road then crosses a beautiful stone road bridge over the Iorsa Water near the conspicuous white house of **Dougarie Lodge**, before continuing towards **Machrie Bay** and crossing Auchencar Bridge. There are many standing stones visible on the moors all along this section, but the best examples are on Machrie Moor, which lies between Machrie and Blackwaterfoot. Walk along the road alongside Machrie Bay, passing a road that leads to the B880 on the left to cross a small road bridge and enter the settlement of **Machrie**. Go past the lovely 9-hole **Machrie Bay golf course** and its clubhouse and tea room. Continue through Machrie, following the road as it sweeps away from the coast, following the course of the Machrie Water. The road then crosses the Machrie Water and gives great views opening out across Machrie Moor and towards Goat Fell. Continue on until you reach the small car park for Machrie Moor Standing Stones. A short distance further along the road is a track to the left, which leads to the **standing stones**.

map continues on page 115

MACHRIE MOOR STANDING STONES

Machrie Moor, considered one of the most important prehistoric sites in Scotland, boasts a fantastic array of standing stones. The site has been used since around 3500BC, when pits were dug on the moor. During excavations Neolithic pottery has been found here and it has now been determined that each of the stone circles on the moor was used as a burial site for the most important people who lived in the area at this time.

The tough miles of road walking are nearly at an end now as you follow the A841 through **Tormore** to reach King's Cave car park. Turn right off the main road and walk through the car park to reach an information board. Turn right here and walk along a good path through a pine forest, passing the site of an old hut circle, one of over 30 that used to be spread across the slopes of **Torr Righ** and Machrie Moor during the Bronze Age.

The path through the forest turns left then right to climb gradually, providing possibly the best view of the whole route – across the sparkling white sands of Machrie Bay and taking in Mullach Buidhe and Goat Fell as well as the blue waters of the Kilbrannan Sound.

The great standing stones on Machrie Moor, the tallest of which stands at 18ft in height

The path then descends gradually, before turning left and continuing above steep slopes beside the forest, where the going is nice and soft underfoot. The steep slopes lead down to the right then descend to reach a cleft in the rock. Here the path twists and turns down through the cleft to reach a gate. Go though the gate and follow the path as it drops steeply down to the shore. Turn left and walk along the stony beach, passing the magnificent King's Cave with Drumadoon Point visible ahead.

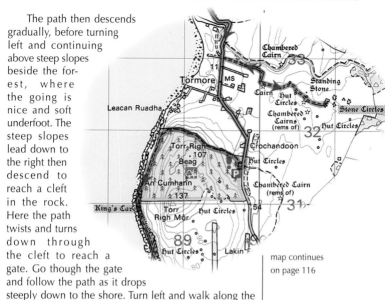

map continues
on page 116

King's Cave is considered one of the possible settings for the story of Robert the Bruce's famed encounter with a determined spider. In the early 14th century the future King of Scots was in hiding and at the depths of despair, having lost a battle as part of his efforts to gain Scottish independence from the occupying forces of England. Deep in thought, he watched as a spider persistently tried to spin its web on the slippy wall of the cave. The web continually collapsed but finally, after many attempts, held. The Bruce was inspired by the spider's determination and decided, at that moment, to continue the fight for his country's freedom. Later, in the 1700s, the cave was used for religious meetings and even as recently as the 19th century it was used as a school.

Walking towards King's Cave, the path climbs high above the coast and gives an exceptional view along Machrie Bay

The beach then gives way to a good path that, past the cave, climbs left away from the rocky shore through undergrowth to reach a fork at a signpost. Take the right-hand fork to pass an Arran Coastal Path arrow and continue above the shore along a good sandy track. Follow the path as it descends over a couple of rocky steps back down to the shore, from where a sandy path continues alongside steep slopes rising to the left. A broad grassy path lined with an abundance of wildflowers (home to colourful butterflies and moths) then makes its way towards **Drumadoon Point** and The Doon. As you approach The Doon you will pass some small yet distinctive stone cairns and then a large boulder. Here the path begins to climb steadily to reach the base of the cliffs below **The Doon**, where it forks.

Turn left to climb the steep path to reach

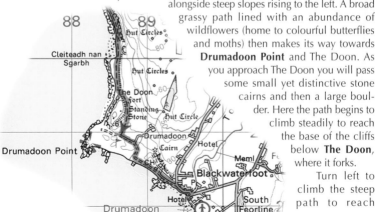

a gate. ▶ Go though and bear right onto a broad grassy path, passing between a couple of old fence posts to continue across a field where there are sheep grazing. Pass through another gate and then keep the fence to the left as you cross the field to reach a gate and stile at **Shiskine golf course**. Arran has several golf courses but Shiskine is unique in that it is one of the world's rare 12-hole courses. It is also often ranked among Britain's top 100 courses.

If you want to climb to the top of The Doon, which is the largest fort on Arran, turn right before the gate and climb the grassy slopes to the top.

Cross the stile and descend the track to the edge of the golf course. Turn left onto a singletrack golf course road, which skirts the edge of the fairways to the right. Follow the road as it passes two big stone gateposts on the left, then crosses a burn. After crossing the burn the path forks; take the left-hand option to keep the edge of the golf course on the right. This path leads down to some golf course buildings and then turns right to pass tennis courts and a bowling green before reaching the golf clubhouse. Walk through the car park to pass the clubhouse and then turn right and walk down a road to reach Shiskine Golf Pro Shop, where the road bears left. Follow it through another car park down towards **Drumadoon Bay**. Turn left out of the car park and walk along the road, passing some lovely stone villas to reach the A841. Bear right onto the pavement and follow it alongside the road. The road continues above the shore alongside the sea wall, passing some houses to the left as it leads into **Blackwaterfoot**. Sweeping round to the left to pass Harbour Shop, it then bears right round the small harbour to cross the bridge over the Black Water. On the other side of the bridge turn right into the car park beside the hotel.

Blackwaterfoot is a small, attractive village near the south of the island. It has its own small harbour that nestles at the foot of the Black Water, hence the village's name. Like many Scottish place names, the original Gaelic is far more poetic: Blackwaterfoot translates from Bun Abhain Dubh. The village sits at the western end of The String road, which was built to link Blackwaterfoot and Brodick by the great Scottish civil engineer and architect Thomas Telford in 1817.

DAY 8
Blackwaterfoot to Kildonan

Start	Car park at Blackwaterfoot NR 895 283
Finish	Kildonan Hotel NS 032 207
Distance	12 miles (19 km)
Time	6 hours
Maps	OS Landranger 69; OS Explorer 361
Terrain	This section, the shortest on Arran in this guide, starts by crossing rough, overgrown paths from Blackwaterfoot to Rinn a'Chrubain. Beautiful stretches of sand, raised beach, roads and pleasant coastal paths lead to Bennan Head. It is crucial to check the tide times here before leaving, as the section of boulder field around Bennan Head is impassable at high tide. Beach, sandy paths and roads conclude the route at Kildonan.
Refreshments	Blackwaterfoot has shops and a hotel and Lagg has an excellent hotel that serves hot meals (see Appendix B). At the time of writing Kildonan Stores is closed but Kildonan Hotel sells refreshments, as does the caravan site adjacent to the hotel.
Public Transport	There is an excellent bus service that runs between Blackwaterfoot and Kildonan. Several buses leave from the former, the times of which coincide with the Brodick to Ardrossan ferry. See Appendix C for details.

The southern section of Arran provides another tough day's walking, with the first and last few miles covering some pretty rough ground. From Blackwaterfoot the route travels along the shore, with much of the path passing over stony, boulder-strewn ground or through overgrown vegetation – however, the nature of the foliage means a vast array of wildflowers grow in abundance along this section. The landscape then opens out to leave the views of Kintyre behind, replaced now by some superb views of the Ayrshire mainland. Paths and tracks along the shore reach a singletrack road that climbs to the A841 at Sliddery.

From here a couple of miles of road walking descend into Lagg and then a path heads back down to the coast, passing the historic Torrylinn Cairn en route. A wonderful section of firm sand leads to the boulder field at Bennan Head, where progress may be slow while you scramble through. This section is impassable at high tide so check the timetables beforehand. The terrain improves past the colossal Black Cave before a combination of beach, shoreline path and road leads into Kildonan, where the wonderful sight of seals basking along the shore is almost guaranteed.

Walk through the car park beside the hotel to reach a singletrack road. Turn left onto it and walk along above the shore, passing several houses on the left. Cross a road entrance on the left and continue straight on, to walk along the road away from **Blackwaterfoot** and pass several more cottages. As the road turns to the

map continues on page 121

left take an indistinct path that bears right through some thicker grass alongside a dry stone dyke.

Follow it past a cottage to lead down onto a stony, rocky shore. The path then forks at an Arran Coastal Way sign. Take the right-hand fork to reach a narrow grassy path running parallel to the shore. The path leads down onto the shore and crosses a narrow burn. The ground is a bit rough here but, with the lower part of the beach being rocky, it is best to stick to the shingly sand at the top.

The beach becomes a bit stonier as it passes some cottages up on the left to cross another burn. Continue along a sandier path over grassland with some further short sections of rocky ground to cross. Keep as far up the beach as you can, below a dyke with

119

As you pass round **Kilpatrick Point** keep an eye out for the Preaching Cave, which was used for worship from the 17th to 19th centuries.

lovely views across to the southern end of Kintyre and back towards Blackwaterfoot. ◄ Cross another burn that leads over more rocky ground beside a dyke. The ground to the left becomes steeper on the approach to **Rubha Garbhard** and the dyke gives way to a fence. At the end of the fence, bear left up off the beach beside some steep, craggy outcrops, to pick up a narrow grassy path and continue along **Brown Head** on the path above the shore.

Pass underneath the cliffs and carefully make your way along a rough path through some thick brambles and bracken, which hide some rocks and boulders underfoot. The path all along this section to Rinn a'Chrubain is very uneven underfoot, with some rocky ground to cover. Much of the path is also overgrown but the way through is, on the whole, pretty obvious. The thickness of the surrounding vegetation can be hazardous at times so real care should be taken and bear in mind that progress may be slow. There are, however, lovely sections of heather and wildflowers running alongside the shore and the high surrounding cliffs are home to ravens, kestrels and buzzards. There are also great views along this section of the route back towards Drumadoon Point. As you continue

Looking back towards Drumadoon Point from Brown Head

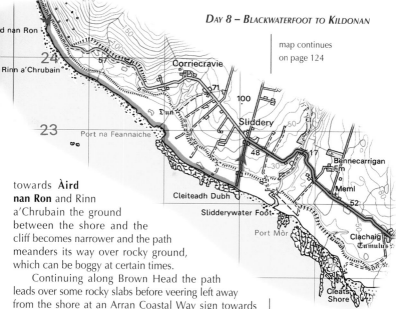

towards **Àird
nan Ron** and Rinn
a'Chrubain the ground
between the shore and the
cliff becomes narrower and the path
meanders its way over rocky ground,
which can be boggy at certain times.

Continuing along Brown Head the path
leads over some rocky slabs before veering left away
from the shore at an Arran Coastal Way sign towards
the cliffs. The path then runs alongside the cliffs, with the
going still rough underfoot. Cross the stile further ahead
back onto the rough, overgrown path, which eventually
leads to **Rinn a'Chrubain** and passes an Arran Coastal Way
sign. The terrain now improves somewhat as it becomes
flatter, grassier ground and it is much more pleasant and
easier to walk along. The hillside climbs gently up towards
the main road and the houses of **Corriecravie** will peak
into view; you will also get the first glimpse of Ailsa Craig
from Arran. A narrow sandy path is then picked up, which
runs alongside the shore. Stay on this path, ignoring the
path that forks away left up into the hillside. The path can
then get a bit boggy and slightly overgrown again as it
passes through more bracken.

Walk along the path beside a low embankment to
the left. ▶ Ignore another path leading to the left, instead
keeping to the shoreline path as it crosses a burn. This
then bears left away from the shore onto a broader path
alongside bracken, leading to a gate at an Arran Coastal

The views of Kintyre
are now left behind
and replaced by
those of the Ayrshire
mainland and Ailsa
Craig.

121

Path sign. Go through the gate and walk along the good path through the bracken to reach a fork just below another gate. Take the right-hand fork and walk along a broad, grassy track underneath the hillside and beside an electric fence. The track continues down to a gate at the entrance to a field. Pass the gate on the left and walk through more bracken, turning left then right to head back down towards the shore. After the bracken the path bears left to run parallel with the coastline.

It then gives way to softer, sandier ground above the beach at **Port na Feannaiche** to reach a fence. Turn left here and walk a short distance to a gatepost, then turn right and go through the gate to follow the path back towards the shore. ◄ The path veers left and continues parallel with the shore, then crosses a burn. Walk along beside an electric fence, keeping it to your left, with views here leading to the remains of the fort of Torr a' Chaisteal.

It may be a bit boggy as it passes through some long grasses.

> **Torr a' Chaisteal**, translated from Gaelic simply as Castle Hill, stands conspicuously above the coast near the scattering of houses at Corriecravie. It houses the remains of an Iron Age fort built around 200AD, which would have been impressive at that time as it had walls between 10ft and 12ft thick and a diameter of 45ft. It would have provided an excellent vantage point along the coast.

Cross another burn and continue beside the fence to a gate beside a distinct rocky outcrop and go through it to reach a boggy path. Cross a section of stony beach and, at the end of the fence, pass a pond to the left. The path merges with a broad farm track here. Join the track as it runs parallel with the shore, passing a couple of further ponds to continue alongside a field containing an old farm building.

When the track turns sharply to the left above **Cleiteadh Dubh** continue straight on through a gate and then bear right down a stony slope towards the shore. Walk towards the end of the beach and, at a rocky outcrop, turn left to make your way away from the beach onto a grassy track leading to a cottage.

The Lagg Hotel, in business since 1791

Walk along the track between two fences to reach a singletrack road at the cottage and an old, disused building. Walk past the buildings and follow the track as it turns left then right, climbing gradually away from the coast to reach the A841 at **Sliddery**.

Turn right at Sliddery Supplies onto the A841 and walk along the verge towards Lagg and Kilmory. ▶ The road travels alongside hedgerows, passing several cottages and farms to descend steeply to a stone bridge crossing the Sliddery Water. After crossing the bridge it climbs, initially steeply and then more steadily, to eventually pass The Ross road at an old church and a war memorial. Continue to walk along the road, passing several more cottages and, on the right, the cart track for **Cleats Shore**. The road then descends steeply down into **Lagg**, passing a signpost for Kilmory, to reach the Lagg Hotel.

There are great views from here across the Firth of Clyde towards Ailsa Craig and the mainland.

THE LAGG HOTEL

The Lagg Hotel, which first opened its doors to the public in 1791, is one of the oldest hostelries on Arran. Little work was done on the hotel for over 150 years until it was extended by its owners, the Crook family, in the 1950s and 60s to include more bedrooms, a kitchen and a dining room. Surrounded by steep slopes, the hotel is very peaceful and little encouragement is required for tired walkers to step inside, relax and refuel.

From the hotel continue along the road to cross a bridge over the Kilmory Water. Just as the road begins to climb out of Lagg, turn right onto a track signposted for the Torrylin Cairn. The track climbs gently through a wood to reach a fork. Take the right-hand fork, which climbs out of the wood onto a grassy path and follows the line of a dry stone wall, giving lovely coastal views as it reaches **Torrylin Cairn**.

> **Torrylin Cairn** is another interesting historic site along the Arran coast. Over 5000 years ago, this was a burial chamber. When first built the cairn internally housed a stone structure of four compartments (the areas where the compartments stood are still visible even today). During an excavation of these areas in 1900 the bones of six adults, a child and a baby were found, mixed together in the innermost compartment. A flint tool, a broken piece of pottery and animal bones were also found.

After visiting the cairn continue along the path, which drops by a fence and some gorse bushes down to a gate. Turn right through the gate at an Arran Coastal Path sign onto an open field and walk down alongside a dyke towards the shore. Just before the shore you will reach a fence and a stile. Cross the stile, walk straight down onto the shore and then turn left. If the tide is out there is a beautiful stretch of firm sand to walk along.

map continues
on page 127

Pladda and Ailsa Craig at dawn from the shore at Kildonan

However, if the tide is in keep to the stony top of the beach. Walk along and enjoy the great views towards **Eilean Mairi**. ▶ Continue on to pass a farmhouse high up on the hillside and then a small, wooden house above the shore. At low tide this is a lovely section of firm sand to walk across that gives glimpses ahead to the small, pear-shaped island of **Pladda**, which lies off the shore at Kildonan.

There are also some lovely smooth stones to be seen along the shore.

PLADDA

Pladda is a prominent marker that, combined with the mass of Ailsa Craig, makes for a fantastic view on the approach to Kildonan. The island rises to only 89ft above sea level and, incredibly, has its own source of fresh water. Pladda is also home to a lighthouse bearing the same name, which was built in 1790 and automated in 1990.

As the end of the beach is approached the ground becomes rockier, so bear left to the top of the beach, reaching a grassy path beside a line of boulders. Walk along the

The awesome scale of the Black Cave dwarfs the walker

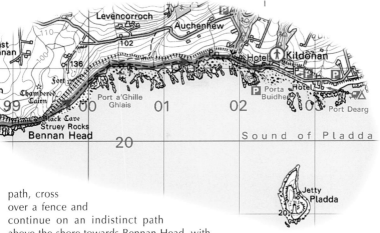

path, cross
over a fence and
continue on an indistinct path
above the shore towards Bennan Head, with
steep cliffs rising to the left. The path continues at the
base of the hillside and crosses a burn to reach a fence.
Turn left though a space in the fence, then turn right and
walk along the grassy path above the beach. The path
continues through some thick ferns and bracken, becoming rougher underfoot but giving fantastic views of the
sheer cliffs at Bennan Head.

Keep to the top of the beach, to the right of the
bracken, to reach a gate and signpost that informs that it
is a further 1.3km to Bennan Head and Black Cave and
4.2km to Kildonan. Go though the gate and follow the
indistinct path above a very rocky beach to reach a stile,
then cross it and walk along another overgrown path.
Although the path is obvious it can also be uneven and
boggy. The route becomes rockier as it leads towards the
cliffs at Bennan Head.

Progress is slow on the approach to Black Cave as
you scramble across great slabs of rocks and boulders
and pass beneath a dramatic waterfall. After crossing a
burn the enormous, incredibly impressive **Black Cave** is
reached, which is impassable at high tide.

127

The fantastic shore at Kildonan is a peaceful spot

After the cave there is no obvious path to take, so it is a matter of scrambling across the boulders underneath the sheer cliffs, keeping high up the beach away from the slippy rocks for a further mile. Kildonan comes into view as you make your way round the shore towards Port a'Ghille Ghlais.

The ground eventually becomes easier (and the boulders smaller) as an indistinct path is picked up. Walk along the rough path underneath the hillside, taking care underfoot despite the path gradually improving as you progress. The path then crosses the beach at Port a'Ghille Ghlais to reach a gate. Go through it and join a broader path above the shore, making sure to look out for seals basking along the bay. Go through another gate, walk along a rough path and then cross a stony beach. Rejoin a grassy path, which leads past the track leading left to **Auchenhew**. Walk along another section of beach onto a good path, passing more lovely waterfalls tumbling from the hillside. Cross a bridge over a burn and then continue along the path towards **Kildonan**.

KILDONAN

Kildonan is named after the Irish monk Saint Donan, who lived here in around the 6th century. The village has a fantastic bay where an abundance of seals relax on the sandy beach and on the rocks; sea otters are also common here. Kildonan has its own castle, which was built in the 13th century by the Lords of the Isles (the powerful nobility who essentially ruled the northern and western seaboards of Scotland between the 10th and 15th centuries) in a prominent position above the village. Today the castle is a ruin but in its heyday, like its counterparts at Brodick and Lochranza, it played an important role in defending attacks from any marauding foes approaching from the Firth of Clyde.

Another sandy bay is crossed, reaching a path that merges with a gravelly path. Go through two gates then turn left onto a singletrack road and pass a few cottages.

Pass a small car park and walk along the singletrack road to meet the road for Kildonan. Turn right here, cross a bridge and then follow the road above the beach, passing several cottages and the village hall. The road then travels above the sea wall to reach the road for the Kildonan Hotel. Turn right here and follow the road past the campsite to reach the **hotel**.

DAY 9
Kildonan to Brodick

Start	Kildonan Hotel NS 032 207
Finish	Brodick Ferry Terminal NS 022 359
Distance	15 miles (24 km)
Time	7 hours
Maps	OS Landranger 69; OS Explorer 361
Terrain	The final day on Arran is a tough one, as some of the route crosses remote shoreline that includes sections of boulder hopping and a little scrambling. Pavements, beach, cycle track and woodland paths make up the rest of the route. Some of the terrain is awkward to cross, which can slow progress and make for quite a long day.
Refreshments	Kildonan Hotel sells refreshments, as does the caravan site adjacent to the hotel. Whiting Bay, Lamlash and Brodick have a vast array of shops, pubs and restaurants.
Public Transport	There is an excellent bus service that runs between Kildonan and Brodick, the times of which coincide with the Brodick to Ardrossan ferry. See Appendix C for details.

The final day on Arran can be both mentally and physically demanding but it is never anything less than breathtaking. The walk between Kildonan and Brodick features remote beaches, spectacular waterfalls and beautiful villages, which really bring to light the variety of scenery Arran has to offer. The toughest part of the day is near the beginning as, after a sedate walk from Kildonan along a sandy then stony beach, the approach to Dippin Head crosses huge boulders and you may need to use your hands and feet here on occasion. It does, however, make for an exciting passage round Dippin Head to the quiet surrounds of Largybeg. Good shoreline paths and pavement lead into Whiting Bay and from here a lovely woodland trail leads to the spectacular Glenashdale Falls. A long section of cycle track through forest then heads into Arran's biggest village, Lamlash. A walk through the village continues to Clauchlands Point and then a rougher path above beautiful clear waters ends near Corriegills Point. A final section along singletrack road passes through North Corriegills, which in turn leads back to Brodick and the ferry back across to the mainland.

At the back of the Kildonan Hotel take the line of stone steps that lead down onto the beach and then turn left to walk along it, passing a small campsite on the left. Here it is best to keep as close to the sea as possible, as the sand is a lot firmer and there are a lot of interesting rocks and boulders sitting on the shore. Continue along the beach, passing cottages and the remains of **Kildonan Castle** on the higher ground above. The sand then gives way to a rockier shore. At the end of the beach bear left to pick up an indistinct sandy path.

The path makes its way along a raised beach. ▶ It is carpeted with an incredible selection of wildflowers (during the spring and summer months in particular) including campion, scurvy grass, and primrose. Keep to the main path as it continues along the shore, crossing a rocky shelf back onto a grassy path. Keep to the top of the shore as you approach Porta Leacach. The path becomes rough underfoot and less distinct here, so take extra care along this slightly awkward section.

Porta Leacach comprises only a few cottages. As you pass them the walking becomes a bit easier as it crosses some flat, rocky shelves. After the last cottage walk up to the top of the beach to reach a narrow, short section of grassy path. This then reverts back to a mixture of rocky shelves and raised beach, both providing good conditions underfoot for walking. However, this is short-lived. As the shore continues towards Dippin Head the walking becomes more awkward as the boulders become bigger.

The shore passes underneath steep cliffs with mixed woodland

There is a path to the left here that leads to Kildonan Castle.

map continues on page 133

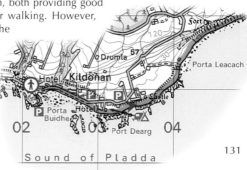

131

hugging the slopes, leading to another section of grassy path along a raised beach with a couple of narrow burns to cross. A section of stony beach then leads to the main boulder field. Progress will be considerably slow all the way round Dippin Head as there are some huge boulders to be dealt with and you will probably have to use your hands at various points. Be careful of the potential for twisted knees and ankles. It is best to stay as high up the beach as you can, as the nearer the sea you are the greater the likelihood that the boulders will be slippy.

The awkwardness of this section can prove both physically and mentally quite demanding, as a high level of concentration is required to cross the boulder field. ◀ Having said that, it is great fun! The boulders are generally flat, allowing you to step from one to the next, and above the tide-line grip is good. The colours of the plant life here such as sea pinks and lichen are fantastic, as are the views back towards Ailsa Craig and Pladda.

As you round Dippin Head the beach becomes narrower between sea and cliff and at very high tides it may be tricky. Continue underneath the great, steep cliffs and enjoy the wonderful views towards **Largybeg Point** and beyond to the distinctive contours of Holy Isle.

If you are planning to catch a ferry back to Ardrossan from Brodick today, ensure you take extra time into account for this section.

The fantastic view of Holy Isle from Largybeg Point

HOLY ISLE

The view of the conspicuous outline of Holy Isle is constant as you walk from Dippin Head to Clauchlands Point past Lamlash. Saint Molaise landed on the island in the 6th century and it was thereafter known as *Eilean Molaise* (Molaise's Island), eventually becoming Holy Isle in the 19th century. There is a cave named after Saint Molaise on the island (so named as it was his chosen place of retreat) and there are also two lighthouses. The island was bought in 1987 by the Buddhist monks of Samye Ling. Holy Isle, under the tutelage of Lama Yeshe, is now a retreat during the summer months. Visitors can take the short boat journey from Lamlash to visit for the day, allowing a walk to Holy Isle's highest point, Mullach Mòr.

The terrain becomes easier as you approach Largybeg Point. Walk along the stony beach above lovely blue waters before bearing left up onto a grassy path just before the first of a few cottages. Pass the cottages, walking alongside an old fence, and then follow the rough track as it heads back down onto the beach. This is a really quiet spot where oystercatchers and seals are abundant.

map continues on page 134

As you approach the final cottage, pass through a gap in the rocks then bear left to climb up onto a raised beach and walk past the cottage. Climb up onto a shelf of red sandstone where there is now a choice of routes. The easiest option is to continue straight on over some rocks and sand, leading to a grass embankment above the beach where a path is picked up for Whiting Bay.

The second option, which gives the finest views, is to turn left from the sandstone shelf and climb very steeply through

a narrow gap in the rocks to reach a fence beside a field. Cross the fence, turn right and walk along a field edge onto an obvious ridge that sweeps round to the right and climbs to a pair of **standing stones**, where you can look along the Firth of Clyde towards Whiting Bay and out to Holy Isle. This is a stunning vantage point that shows the coast at its finest.

Retrace your steps from the standing stones for a short distance to reach a path. Turn right onto it as it descends back down towards the shore. Walk along the sandy path above the shore, which narrows as it makes its way through gorse and past a large cliff face. ◄ Continue past woodland before the path peters out as a stile is approached.

If the track is too muddy here it may be best to walk along the stony beach instead.

map continues on page 138

Cross the stile and then a second stile that takes you into a field. Keep to the right edge of the field, which runs above the shore. There may be cattle grazing here. A narrow burn is then crossed before the field edge continues past some cottages near **Largymore**.

Cross another stile and continue along the field edge to pass a large red sandstone house, then cross a narrow burn followed by another stile. Turn left then immediately right to go through a gate. Turn right onto the A841 just before Whiting Bay.

WHITING BAY

From a scattering of cottages near the shore the village of Whiting Bay began to grow in the 18th century when the construction of a pier brought in more trade. The area is very rich in history; many pre-historic relics have been found here as well as evidence of the Viking occupation at a nearby burial ground at Kingscross. It has been suggested that Whiting Bay comes from the Old Norse *Hvit Ting*, which translates as White Place of Assembly, but it is more likely that the name derives from the proliferation of whiting that was to be found in the seas around the coast. Whiting Bay, along with Kilmory and Lochranza, was closely linked with the whisky smuggling trade during the 18th and 19th centuries. The village today has a good variety of services, shops and restaurants as well as a challenging 18-hole golf course.

There is no pavement at this point, so walk carefully along the road, passing a sea wall to reach a grass verge. Walk along above the shore into **Whiting Bay**, passing some bungalows as you enter the village. The verge then gives way to a pavement, which continues round by another sea wall and then passes a caravan park on the left-hand side of the road. Walk by the caravan park and, just before a road bridge, cross the A841 opposite a single-track road signposted for **Glenashdale Falls**.

Make your way up the road as it climbs gradually into lovely mixed woodland, with the **Glenashdale Burn** below on the right. The road passes several cottages. After the last, continue straight on by an open fence where the road narrows to a path. Continue through this slice of glorious woodland for 100m to reach a fork in the path. Take the right-hand fork signposted for Glenashdale Falls and walk along the path through more woodland. This section really emphasises the diversity of Arran's coastal path, as it quickly moves from boulder field and rugged coastline to beautiful, peaceful woodland and dramatic waterfalls.

The path begins to climb quite steeply before crossing a burn via a wooden footbridge. It then zigzags its way up through the wood to flatten out high above the gorge and the Glenashdale Burn. Cross another wooden footbridge, turning right at a signpost for Glenashdale Falls before

The spectacular Glenashdale Falls

continuing into pine forest. The path begins to climb very steeply, reaching two flights of wooden steps that lead to a wooden platform giving a spectacular view of the falls.

Retrace your steps from the platform and then immediately turn right onto a path. This then turns to the right to cross a wooden footbridge over a burn and reach a fork. Take the right-hand fork signposted Whiting Bay and Iron Age Fort and walk through the trees with Glenashdale Falls now dropping away to your right. Cross two wooden bridges and continue to reach a forest clearing at a waymarked signpost, then turn right and walk down a narrow path to another post. Follow the path as it veers round to the right and passes through a gap in a wall. It then gradually descends through the forest to another small clearing. This is home to an **Iron Age fort** that is estimated to be 2000–2500 years old.

Continue past the fort along the woodland path that bears left down to a footbridge crossing a burn. The path then swings right, making its way to a flight of wooden steps. Climb the steps to reach a signpost for Whiting Bay. The path now turns sharply left and climbs steeply past a waymarked sign to reach a broad forestry road. A signpost points right for Whiting Bay but ignore this; instead turn left to climb steadily up the road as it swings round to the right to reach the broad Kilmory cycle track. Turn right onto the track, which gradually climbs and provides excellent views of Whiting Bay and Holy Isle. ▶

Swinging to the left, the track gives further great views over **Whiting Bay golf course** and the Firth of Clyde to the Ayrshire mainland. Continue to follow as it enters a forest, which sadly eliminates the surrounding expansive views although at certain points, as the descent is made towards The Ross road, the forest has been cleared and the views towards Goat Fell are amazing. The walking is easy here and there is a variety of wildflowers and birdlife to see, such as the wild rose and the blue tit. Several Forestry Commission tracks lead away from the main track but ignore these and keep to the cycle track.

As you near The Ross road, there is a path that bears left from the main track leading to Meallach's Grave, which is a small Neolithic chambered cairn. Excavations in 1902 and 1961 found fragments of pottery and flint here. It is a short walk to the cairn if you wish to visit it. Continue to descend the cycle track as it steepens before flattening to cross a wooden bridge over a river. It then passes a small car park to the left and continues to meet The Ross road. Turn right out of the forest onto the singletrack road and walk alongside a burn and woodland towards Lamlash. Pass the turning for Glenkiln Farm and the Arran Fine

This section of today's route along the cycle track continues for around three miles to reach The Ross road on the outskirts of **Lamlash**.

Foods factory and shop to reach the A841. Turn left here and walk along the pavement towards **Lamlash**.

With a population of around 1100, **Lamlash** is the largest settlement on Arran. It is home to many important buildings, including the island's hospital, secondary school and local government offices. Lamlash was called Kirktoun of Kilbride in around the 14th century but later took the name Eilean Molaise. The name of the island across the bay was anglicised to become Holy Isle (shown on the OS map as Holy Island), whereas the village kept the Gaelic variant of the name and this gradually became Lamlash at the beginning of the 19th century. King Hakon IV of Norway took shelter here after his defeat at by Alexander III of Scotland at the Battle of Largs in 1263 while, more recently, the bay was used as a naval base during both World Wars. The village holds a fantastic position right on the coast and

map continues
on page 143

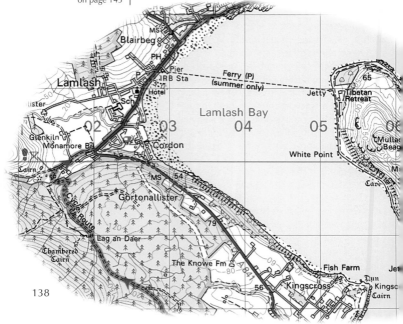

it gives superb views to Holy Isle as well as across to the mainland. Tourists who come to Lamlash (particularly to sail and golf) play a major role in the village's economy.

The jagged outline of Goat Fell rising above Lamlash

Continue along past several houses and when the pavement ends cross to the right-hand side of the road to walk along past the fire station. The pavement ends near a sign for **Cordon**. Cross back over to the left-hand side of the road and continue, crossing a side street and then a road bridge that crosses the Benlister Burn. Another side street is then crossed before you reach Arran High School on the left and the police station on the right. The pavement continues, passing Arran's coastguard station and some tennis courts to head into Lamlash village centre.

After passing **Lamlash Church** cross to the right-hand side of the road and walk along either the pavement or the section of open parkland above the shore. Continue to the end of

07
HOLY
ISLAND

Pillar Rock Point

A stunning sunrise over Holy Isle from Lamlash

It is interesting to watch the ever-changing profile of Holy Isle as you make your way round Lamlash Bay towards Clauchlands Point.

the parkland and then bear left onto the pavement. Cross the exit and entrance to a car park and then pass a children's play park and the **RNLI Lifeboat Station**. Cross the side street that leads down to Lamlash harbour (where you can catch the ferry to Holy Isle) and walk along the pavement to pass Lamlash Bowling Club and another side street.

The A841 now sweeps round to the left away from Lamlash to head towards Brodick but ignore the turn and continue straight on towards Clauchlands Point along the minor road that runs parallel to the shore. ◄ There is no pavement here so walk along the side of the road to pass some impressive large villas. The road then crosses a bridge and passes a side road that leads to Arran War Memorial Hospital. As you continue to walk towards Clauchlands Point there is a very good chance of seeing seals in the water and along the shore. The road then narrows to become a singletrack road that passes a track to the left signposted for Dun Fionn and Brodick.

Follow the shore, passing a signpost for Clauchlands Point and Brodick. Walk along the singletrack road, passing the Arran Outdoor Education Centre on the left and

A rare occurrence – snow on the beach at Lamlash

its car park on the right to reach a small car park at the road end.

Lamlash has been at the forefront of attempts to pre-serve the fantastic marine life that exists along its shores. The **Community of Arran Seabed Trust (COAST)** was set up in 1995 by two local divers to regenerate fish and scallop populations and to enhance the marine biodiversity in Lamlash Bay through the creation of Scotland's first No Take Zone which, after years of polit-ical campaigning by the trust, was finally established in 2008. The No Take Zone means that no marine life can be removed by any method or for any purpose.

Passing the entrance of **Clauchlands Farm**, go through a wooden gate onto a broad sandy track and walk along it beside the shore to reach **Clauchlands Point**. There is a seat at the point where you can take a rest and admire the wonderful views across the sea to the Ayrshire mainland and back to Lamlash. There is an extensive range of birdlife here that includes shags, gulls and oystercatchers.

From Clauchlands Point continue along the track, ignoring a broader track that climbs away to the left. Instead walk round the point, as it turns to the left, onto a rough path that continues through scrubby grass above the shore to reach a stile. ◄ Cross it and climb the path, which gives a sumptuous view right along the coast towards Brodick Bay as well as to the bare, rocky slopes of Goat Fell that rise steeply to its conical summit. The path then narrows to continue above the shore beneath steep slopes rising to the left. The waters are crystal clear here and the rocks on the seabed are clearly visible. The rough path continues its journey along the coast to reach a fork. Take the left-hand path as it leads away from the shore over some rockier ground before heading back down towards the shore.

Approaching Corriegills Point the path is a bit rough and boggy so progress may be slow. However, stepping stones and wooden planks have been laid over the boggiest

Keep an eye out for the Caledonian MacBrayne ferry as it crosses the Firth of Clyde.

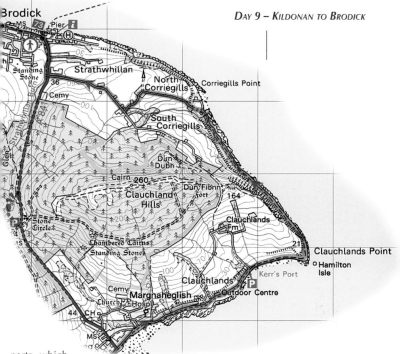

parts, which
is a considera-
ble help. The path improves as you cross a narrow burn to
reach a fence and a broad stile. Cross the stile and walk
along the path, passing wooded slopes and continuing
alongside red sandstone slabs that cross a shallow burn.
A good, firm path continues towards Corriegills Point and
the scattering of houses at Dunan. Cross a small, sandy
beach to reach Dunan and then walk past a house, cross
a burn and continue onto a singletrack road that reaches
a fork.

Turn left here onto another singletrack road, which
climbs away from the coast to pass a few more cottages.
The road continues quite steeply alongside hedgerows
towards North Corriegills. Ignore the track to the right,
which leads to a radio mast, and instead follow the road

143

A rugged path above a fantastic stretch of coastline from Clauchlands Point towards Brodick Bay

as it swings sharply to the left to pass some more houses before reaching a road junction at North Corriegills.

Turn right onto the singletrack road, which proceeds past a few more cottages and provides yet more fantastic views of Arran's mountains, with Brodick Castle dwarfed at their base. Walk along the road as it passes a couple of cottages and a Scottish Water plant and then descends steeply through lovely countryside to reach the A841. Turn right and cross some driveways to reach the pavement. Walk alongside the road, crossing the side road for Strathwhillan, and continue straight on to head towards the ferry terminal. Turn right into the ferry terminal and pass the tourist information centre. Now cross the road opposite the Caledonian MacBrayne ticket office to take the last few steps on Arran to reach the ferry gangway.

DAY 10
Ardrossan to Largs

Start	Ardrossan Ferry Terminal NS 224 422
Finish	Largs Ferry Terminal NS 201 595
Distance	15 miles (24 km)
Time	5 hours
Maps	OS Landranger 70 and 63; OS Explorer 341
Terrain	Mostly flat with no steep climbs. It is relatively easy walking along beach, grassy tracks and short sections of pavement.
Refreshments	Ardrossan, West Kilbride, Fairlie and Largs all have a good selection of shops, pubs, and restaurants.
Public Transport	There are regular train and bus services between Ardrossan and Largs (both stop at West Kilbride and Fairlie en route). See Appendix C for details. Largs railway station (services also include Glasgow) is on Main Street.

The 15 miles between Ardrossan and Largs are pretty straightforward, as much of the walking is predominantly along the beach and grassy tracks. After passing Portencross and its castle the route continues through the nuclear Hunterston B Power Station where no diversion away from the designated path is to be made, for obvious reasons. In sharp contrast to the power station, next comes the quiet town of Fairlie. The route leads on to the outskirts of Kelburn Country Centre and then past busy Largs Marina and The Pencil, which is a monument built to commemorate the famous Battle of Largs in 1263. The route then continues on its way into the bustling town of Largs.

From Ardrossan Ferry Terminal, walk along Harbour Road to the junction with Princes Street, then turn left into Ardrossan's **Marina** and follow the pavement round by some attractive apartments to reach Ardrossan's harbour. Upon reaching a waymarked signpost continue along the pavement out of the marina and away from the harbour to reach another waymarked signpost. Bear left here into a short section of open waste ground. This is an old industrial site (now waiting to be redeveloped), which has a line of barbed wire fencing to the right of the path.

map continues
on page 149

Although the route here is obvious the ground underneath can be a bit uneven so take care. Once out of the site turn left onto the pavement beside the A78 main road and then bear left onto an indistinct grassy path that leads down onto the beach at **North Bay**, where there are fantastic views of Arran as well as of the iconic Caledonian MacBrayne ferry leaving and entering the harbour. Continue towards Seamill along the wide, sandy beach, which offers tremendous walking and is a great place to spot oystercatchers and dunlins.

As you approach Seamill, the beach gives way to sand dunes and a grassy path at **South Inch**, which makes its way round the perimeter fence of a small caravan park.

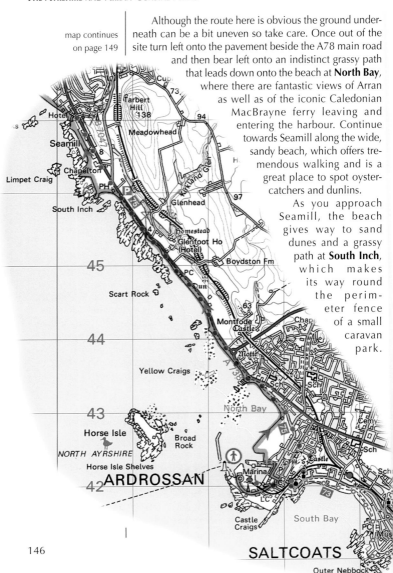

Pass a waymarked signpost and continue along the grassy track to reach another signpost, which points the way to lead up from the beach onto a grassy track. Carry on towards Seamill and pass a row of houses at **Chapelton**. After the houses, take the path to the left that leads back onto the sand. Walk along the beach, cross a burn by a stone bridge and continue along to enjoy the great views along the coast in all directions.

Ardrossan's Marina, seen here at dawn, is home to a great number of yachts

The boundaries between **Seamill** and **West Kilbride** are now blurred due to their expansion towards each other but they are two separate villages in their own right. Seamill, the smaller of the two, was named after one of its oldest buildings, the local water-driven mill. It is probably best known for the renowned Seamill Hydro, which opened in 1880 as the equivalent of a present-day health spa and subsequently became popular for its therapeutic qualities. It is now a hotel and popular wedding venue.

West Kilbride hails itself as Scotland's 'Craft Town' due to its abundance of craft shops and galleries. There is evidence of settlement in the area from around 82AD,

147

The beach near Seamill features huge boulders and gives stunning views across to Arran

but it began to expand when several buildings were constructed in the medieval period. The prominent Law Castle was built in the village in the 15th century. It took some 50 years to complete and was built for Mary, the daughter of King James II. The town flourished in the 19th century due to its five mills, which produced oats and flax.

Pass Seamill Hydro and a high sea defence wall then, at a waymarked signpost, climb from the beach onto a grassy track. This gives way to a flat, stony track that continues above the beach alongside **West Kilbride golf course**; the path and golf course separated by a wall. Walk along the track and, at the northern end of the golf course, follow it as it sweeps round to the right to meet with the B7048 opposite **Ardneil Farm**.

Turn left and walk along the pavement to pass **Ardneil Bay** and head towards **Portencross**, which consists of only a few houses, a small castle and a lovely little harbour. When you reach Portencross walk past a car park. Turn left after the car park and walk down the singletrack road to reach the castle.

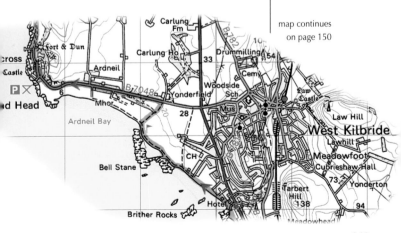

map continues
on page 150

map continues
on page 153

Holding a prominent position near Farland Head, **Portencross Castle** rises impressively above the small village of Portencross. The original castle stood on Auld Hill before it was moved in around the 14th century and rebuilt at today's site. King Robert II signed many Royal Charters here during his lifetime, while it is believed that the bodies of several Scottish kings were taken to Portencross Castle so that they could be transported to Iona for burial. A charitable company called the Friends of Portencross Castle was formed in 1998 to protect the castle's future. Restoration work began in 2007 with construction completed in September 2010 and it is now open to the public, with seasonal opening times. See **www. portencrosscastle.org.uk** for details.

Continue along the B7048 to reach a metal gate at the road end. Turn left through the gate and onto a grassy track that leads past the small but lovely harbour away from Portencross, with good views extending towards The Cumbraes, Millport and the Cowal Peninsula.

The grassy path then merges with a stony track. Keep on this track as it passes a driveway to a house and some impressive cliffs. At a metal gate the first views of the nuclear Hunterston B Power Station lie ahead. Pass through the gate and walk along the track onto a pavement and stay on it as it travels through the site, which has many signs that bring to your attention the dangers that lie within the area.

Although the high metal fencing that surrounds the plant keeps you well away from any hazards, do not divert away from the pavement at any time. It is only a short walk through but this is a section of today's route that markedly contrasts with the sheer beauty of the Ayrshire Coastal Path. Fortunately, it does not take long to leave Hunterston B behind.

Once away from the plant pass a road to the left (which leads to a construction site) and then as the road splits at a metal gate take the left-hand fork that leads towards the A78, passing **Gull's Walk**. ▶ Carry on along this road until you meet a waymarked signpost.

Bear left onto a track that takes you through a line of trees to the A78, just north of a roundabout. Turn left and walk along the pavement (also a National Cycle Track), which provides pleasant walking through some short stretches of woodland. The woods conceal the main road and there are great views here towards Kaim Hill.

At the next roundabout near **Southannan Sands**, which has a sign for Clydeport, cross the road and continue north along the A78 into **Fairlie**, passing some fine bungalows along the way. Turn left onto a side road and walk along to reach a picnic area.

The impressive **Hunterston House**, an attractive private residence, sits away to your right.

The setting sun just manages to peek through the cloud over a peaceful, calm Fairlie

FAIRLIE

Fairlie was only a small fishing village until, with the arrival of the railway in the 19th century, more people started to move to the village and it began to flourish. With the opening of the two Hunterston nuclear power stations in 1964 and 1976 respectively, it continued to grow. Much of the village sits just above the coast and it is blessed with remarkable views of the Ayrshire coast. It has good amenities including several shops and a post office. In 2005 Fairlie became Scotland's first Fairtrade Village, thereby committing itself to supporting Fairtrade and using products bearing the Fairtrade logo.

After passing the picnic area and public toilets the road converges with a path and crosses a bridge onto the beach. Here a cemented path runs alongside the beach with a sea wall to the right. ◀ The path then climbs above the shoreline, passing the back gardens of a line of houses. A line of stone steps at the end of the row descends left to the shore.

At high tide your feet may get wet here.

ALTERNATIVE

If the tide is very high ignore the steps and, instead, at the last of the houses turn right into a narrow lane, which climbs gradually up to the A78. On reaching the main road, turn left and walk along the pavement to Fairlie Parish Church and then cross Pier Road to continue north along the A78.

If the tide is low enough then descend the steps left to reach the shoreline. Turn right to continue along the sandy beach and at the end of the sea wall climb a flight of steps to the right that take you onto Bay Street. Turn left and walk along the street until you reach a small car park on the right. Turn into the car park and climb a flight of steps to reach a waymarked sign at Fairlie Parish Church, then cross Pier Road to turn left onto the A78.

map continues
on page 154

▶ If the tide is too high and you have continued along pavement, rejoin the main route here.

Walk a short distance along the A78 to a waymarked sign. Carefully cross the main road, turn left onto the pavement and walk north past a garage. Continue on to reach the entrance of **Kelburn Country Centre**, which is well worth a visit as it holds some good woodland walks, lovely plants and animals (including wild garlic, bluebells and red squirrels) and an interesting castle. The castle dates from as far back as the 13th century but in 2007 the facade of its south side took on a very modern look, being transformed by a large-scale Brazilian graffiti project.

153

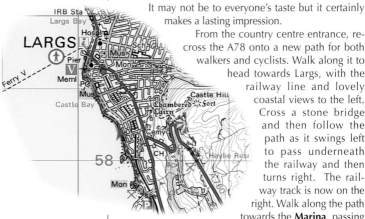

It may not be to everyone's taste but it certainly makes a lasting impression.

From the country centre entrance, re-cross the A78 onto a new path for both walkers and cyclists. Walk along it to head towards Largs, with the railway line and lovely coastal views to the left. Cross a stone bridge and then follow the path as it swings left to pass underneath the railway and then turns right. The railway track is now on the right. Walk along the path towards the **Marina**, passing several interesting old anchors lining the path. Upon reaching the main Marina buildings cross the entrance road and follow the path round the beach towards the distinctive monument, The Pencil.

Autumn waterfall at Kelburn Country Centre

The Pencil at the southern end of Largs, a monument to the 1263 Battle of Largs

THE PENCIL

As you approach Largs you can't help but notice the conspicuous cylindrical monument known as The Pencil, which was built in 1912 to commemorate the 1263 Battle of Largs. The most famous battle in the long running Scottish-Norwegian War ended in a victory for the Scots against King Hakon IV and was instrumental in bringing an end to Viking rule along Scotland's west coast. Every year, in August and September, the Largs Viking Festival celebrates the Viking heritage of the town. Much more can be learnt about the exploits of the Vikings in Scotland at the Vikingar! visitor attraction, which is on Greenock Road in Largs.

A good tarmac path runs alongside the shore and heads past The Pencil towards a block of apartments, before it merges with the promenade. It is now a simple matter of following the promenade above the shoreline, where distinctive coloured benches and some great sandstone villas are passed on the right, as is the Curlinghall Stone. The promenade then carries on by **Castle Bay** onto Fort Street to reach Largs Ferry Terminal.

The **Curlinghall Stone** is a standing stone that can be seen on an area of grassland to the right, as you approach Fort Street. It dates from the Neolithic Period, in which these types of stones, or monoliths, were positioned to mark a significant boundary, meeting point or the burial place of an important person. It is thought that in 1823 Dr John Cairnie, who owned and lived at nearby Curling Hall, placed the stone here. Local belief, however, asserts that the stone actually marks the site of the Battle of Largs (extremely plausible as it is a stone's throw from The Pencil) while another account states that the stone is a memorial to a high-ranking Norwegian soldier who was killed during the fight.

The sport of curling had an integral role in Cairnie's life and in 1813 he established Curlinghall, which was the first indoor curling club in the world. He also played a significant part in establishing the Grand Caledonian Curling Club in 1838, becoming its first President in that year. In 1843 Queen Victoria granted its present title of The Royal Caledonian Curling Club and it has since been described as the mother club of curling.

Largs has many colourful benches along its promenade

DAY 11
Largs to Skelmorlie

Start	Largs Ferry Terminal NS 201 595
Finish	Station Road Skelmorlie NS 194 683
Distance	7 miles (11km) via Low Road; 9 miles (14.5 km) via High Road
Time	3 hours via Low Road; 4 hours via High Road
Maps	OS Landranger 63; OS Explorer 341
Terrain	The walk from Largs to Skelmorlie uses promenade, pavements and minor roads, with a middle section across farmland, open moorland and woodland. There is a short, steep ascent and descent from The Knock although this is avoided on the Low Road variant.
Refreshments	There are several shops, restaurants and pubs in both Largs and Skelmorlie.
Public Transport	Largs railway station (services including Glasgow) is on Main Street. Wemyss Bay railway station, only a short walk from the north end of Skelmorlie, also has regular services for Glasgow. There is a bus back to Largs available from Shore Road in Skelmorlie. See Appendix C for details.

The final day of the Ayrshire Coastal Path is a short walk that offers a choice of two routes from Largs: the Low Road or the High Road (both routes meet three miles south of Skelmorlie). Your remaining fitness levels after the past 10 days of walking may mean the decision makes itself! The Low Road takes you on a more leisurely route along pavement and singletrack road and is a very pleasant walk that provides great views. For the more adventurous the High Road steers itself away from Largs into open, peaceful countryside. On its way to The Knock, the path then passes through a farm where dogs must be kept on leads at all times. Despite being only 712ft in height, The Knock provides a spectacular view along the Ayrshire coast as well as across the Firth of Clyde towards the Cumbraes and Arran. The busy A78 road has to be crossed and then re-crossed at certain points on this route, where extra care should be taken.

Prior to beginning the walk at the ferry terminal the short trip to Great Cumbrae (several ferries leave Largs for the island every day) is highly recommended. Great Cumbrae has several places of interest including

Britain's smallest cathedral, The Cathedral of the Isles, and Garrison House, a former military barracks. Millport, the island's main town, has many shops, beaches, restaurants, and pubs. Great Cumbrae also has many fine walks in and around the island.

Largs translates from the Gaelic *An Leargaidh Ghallda*, which means hillside (in reference to the steep slopes that rise behind the town). It is most identified with the Battle of Largs that took place here in 1263. The town has many historical places of interest including the Haylie Chambered Cairn, which shows that its history extends way back as far as the Neolithic Period. The cairn, which houses the remains of an ancient tomb dating from around 3000BC, sits near the entrance of Douglas Park.

map continues on page 165

More recently Largs became a major tourist destination and during its heyday in the 1960s and 70s thousands of holidaymakers would descend on the town during Glasgow's Fair Fortnight. Due to its proximity to Glasgow and its superb public transport links, many people still visit (especially day-trippers) and regular trips to Great Cumbrae and the calling of the iconic

Waverley at the pier – the last sea-going paddle steamer in the world that carries passengers – are extremely popular. Largs also has a variety of excellent shops, pubs and restaurants.

From the ferry terminal the route heads north along the promenade at **Largs Bay** to pass the RNLI Station and, on reaching a waymarked signpost, the promenade joins Aubrey Park. The walking here is easy along a pavement that travels clockwise round between the small boating pond and the outflow of the Noddsdale Water, leading to the A78. Here a waymarked signpost points left for Skelmorlie by the Low Road and right for Skelmorlie via the High Road.

ALTERNATIVE

For the Low Road turn left out of Aubrey Park, carefully cross the A78 and then turn right into Routenburn Road (known locally as the Low Road), which climbs gradually past some houses. Once across Kelvin Walk the road sweeps round to the left and climbs past **Routenburn golf course**. Although called the Low Road, it actually climbs high above the coast and subsequently the surrounding views of the Cumbraes, Arran, the Ayrshire coast and the Southern Highlands are spectacular. The singletrack road climbs steadily past a farm and then through some sections of mixed woodland before descending past the entrance of **Knock Castle**. It continues through more mixed woodland and then down to meet the junction with the High Road at a waymarked signpost. To continue, see page 164.

For the High Road, carefully cross the busy A78 and turn right then turn left into Barr Crescent. Follow the pavement to pass through the leafy suburbs of Largs. Barr Crescent leads into Noddleburn Road and continues past Noddleburn Meadow to reach a waymarked signpost. Turn left here and follow a lane, which runs beside mixed woodland and the Noddsdale Water to the left and houses to the right. The lane continues to

Viking sculpture at Largs seafront

reach Glen Avenue. Turn left and continue to a way-marked signpost.

At the signpost turn left into Brisbane Glen Road and onto a pavement leading to Brisbane Lodge, which crosses Noddle Bridge and the Noddsdale Water, where the pavement ends.

NOTABLE RESIDENTS OF LARGS

At Noddle Bridge stands a plaque to commemorate **Sir William Thomson** (1824-1907), who became Lord Kelvin of Largs. Born in Belfast, he moved to Glasgow as a child and then Largs in his later years, building and living at Netherhall House. He was a genius in the fields of mathematics and physics and is acknowledged as developing the basis of absolute zero as a measurement of temperature; the Kelvin scale is named after him for the work he did. Such was his standing among his contemporaries and the importance of the work he produced, he was buried in Westminster Abbey next to Sir Isaac Newton.

Another of Largs' most distinguished former residents is **Sir Thomas MakDougall Brisbane**, who was born at Brisbane House in Largs in 1773. After an education in astronomy and mathematics at Edinburgh University he had a distinguished career in the British Army, serving under the Duke of Wellington. Wellington himself then recommended MakDougall to become the 6th Governor of New South Wales in 1821. Such was the impression made by MakDougall on the people of Australia that Brisbane River was named after him (the present-day city subsequently took its name from the river). During the four years he spent in Australia his love of astronomy continued (he had built an observatory in Largs in 1808) and he catalogued more than 7000 stars during this time. He returned to Britain in 1825 and was elected President of the Royal Society of Edinburgh in 1832. Over the years the observatory he built fell into disrepair, but its remains can still be seen on Green Hill near Waterside Street, just a short distance from the town centre.

After crossing the bridge the walk continues along the minor road, which climbs gradually to leave Largs behind. The landscape becomes more peaceful here and there are great views of the steep-sided hills ahead. Pass Brisbane Lodge and, after around 200m, reach another waymarked sign that points left and indicates that The Knock is two miles away. Turn left from Brisbane Glen Road onto a farm track towards **Brisbane Mains Farm**, which gives good walking and a surrounding landscape consisting of very pleasant farmland and woodland.

As the track sweeps to the left it crosses a bridge over the Noddsdale Water, then immediately turns to the right to present fine views of the pointed summit of The Knock. A gate is reached signposted for Brisbane Mains before the track begins to gradually climb to the farm, which is a great white building with quite an unusual architectural style.

Walk round the front of the farm to another wooden gate and then carry on past the building through another gate. The track now becomes grassier and climbs between hedgerows to another gate. ◄ It crosses a small burn then continues past hawthorn and beech trees to a corrugated iron fence. A waymarked signpost at the fence points right onto a narrow path. Keeping the fence to the left, walk to its end to reach a wooden gate. Go through and turn right onto a grassy track, which climbs gradually to a small wooded glen. Continue to reach a small marker post that has a red arrow pointing left towards The Knock.

It can be very boggy underfoot here for a short distance.

The path continues along an easy gradient with open moorland on both sides, which is boggy after prolonged periods of rain. A waymarked post and a line of beech and hawthorn trees are then passed, before the path maintains its course to traverse the slopes of The Knock and meet another waymarked post, where it splits. Bear left and follow the upper path, which traverses The Knock round to the south and gives easy (but boggy) walking. The views begin to open up here across the Firth of Clyde to the Cowal Peninsula, as well as north towards Skelmorlie.

Pass another waymarked signpost as the path climbs gradually to the base of The Knock. It is now just a short, sharp climb to the top. Another path bears left and runs round The Knock, providing an easier climb to the top.

The stunning viewpoint across the Firth of Clyde to Arran from the summit of The Knock

THE KNOCK

The views from The Knock back to Largs, along to Skelmorlie and across the Firth of Clyde to Bute, the Cowal Peninsula and Arran are, quite simply, stunning. Its 712ft summit features the remains of an Iron Age fort; its isolated position and 360° panorama would have made it an ideal location for such a structure. Although the fort is prehistoric, the path leading to the summit is not (having been built in the 19th century by a local landowner so he could ride his horse to the top). The remains of the fort's turf-covered wall are still visible, with some sections rising to around one metre in height. Vitrified rock has also been found in and around The Knock, which has led to the conclusion that the timber framework of the fort, which had huge blocks of stone constructed around it, was either deliberately (possibly by enemy attack) or accidentally set alight, causing the structure to burn with such intense heat that it vitrified the stone into the glassy rock found on the summit.

To descend The Knock, retrace the path back to its base and then follow it down to the waymarked signpost. Turn left here and walk a short distance across open moorland to reach a dry stone dyke. ▶ Turn right and follow the wall for around 200m to a wooden gate directly beside

Take care here as there is no specific path and the ground underneath can be boggy and uneven.

a metal gate and a waymarked signpost. Go through the gates to reach a grassy path that descends past a line of beech trees. Initially the route is unclear and boggy, with no definite path, but keep the small burn to the right and descend west towards a wooded section where the path becomes visible and descends gently towards a gate. The walking is very pleasant here, with oak and beech trees lining the route. Through the gate, the path descends steeply to the Red Road to meet a waymarked signpost.

▶ If you have taken the Low Road alternative, rejoin the main route here.

The signpost here points towards Skelmorlie and shows that the destination of today's walk is three miles away. The following singletrack road provides gentle, easy walking and lovely views opening out across the Firth of Clyde. There are no pavements on this stretch, so take care all the way along it. Walk along the road as it climbs past the farm of **Millrig**. Continue for another mile (with Skelmorlie now in sight) before dropping down past the hamlet of **Meigle**

Sunshine breaks through the clouds near Skelmorlie

and back to the A78. Cross the road (take care as it is extremely busy here with fast-moving traffic), turn right and walk along the short stretch of pavement to a waymarked sign. Re-cross the A78 here to reach a singletrack road.

Walk up the singletrack road (again there is no pavement) and, as it climbs steeply past the imposing red sandstone building of **Skelmorlie Castle**, there are a couple of tight bends. The gradient of the road becomes easier as it climbs past **Skelmorlie Mains Caravan Park** and with the landscape opening out in all directions the views continue to inspire. Past the caravan park continue to walk along the road, passing under a lovely avenue of beech trees to lead into **Upper Skelmorlie** on Skelmorlie Castle Road, which is lined with Victorian sandstone villas. The pavement then descends through Upper Skelmorlie to meet Station Road. Turn right here for a short, steep descent towards the shore at **Skelmorlie** and the end of the Ayrshire Coastal Path.

Wemyss Bay railway station is only a very short walk from the north end of Skelmorlie, or a bus back to Largs is available from Shore Road (see Appendix C for details).

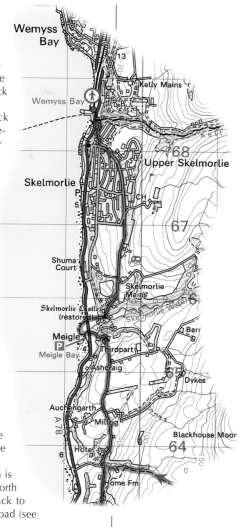

Storm clouds and sunshine accentuate the rugged coastline near Skelmorlie at the end of the Ayrshire and Arran Coastal Paths

Skelmorlie is right on the border between Ayrshire and Renfrewshire, and it has a history that dates back to the 16th century. Its castle was built in 1502 and was the stronghold of the Montgomery Clan. Sir Robert Montgomery built the elaborate Skelmorlie Aisle in Largs in 1636 and both he and his wife are buried there. Its sumptuous and lavish interior, with its wonderfully carved tombstones and ornate design, is completed in spectacular fashion by its incredible ceiling, which was beautifully (and surely painstakingly) illustrated by the artist J.S. Stalker in 1638.

The village was home to several Glasgow tea barons in the latter half of the 19th century and, like Seamill, it was also used as a centre of hydrotherapy at this time. Sitting right on the Firth of Clyde, this peaceful, attractive village provides an extremely satisfying end to the Ayrshire and Arran Coastal Paths.

APPENDIX A

Route summary table

Day	Start	Finish	Distance	Time	Maps	Page No
1	Glenapp	Ballantrae	8½ miles (13.5km)	4 hours	OS Landranger 76; OS Explorer 317	25
2	Ballantrae	Girvan	13 miles (21km)	5 hours	OS Landranger 76; OS Explorer 317 and 326	35
3	Girvan	Dunure	14 miles (23km)	6 hours	OS Landranger 76 and 70; OS Explorer 326	46
4	Dunure	Troon	18 miles (29km)	7 hours	OS Landranger 70; OS Explorer 326	61
5	Troon	Ardrossan	Main route: 17 miles (27km); alternative via Dundonald Castle: 27 miles (43km)	Main: 6 hours; alternative: 9½ hours	OS Landranger 70; OS Explorer 326 333 and 341	78
6	Brodick	Lochranza	16 miles (26km)	7 hours	OS Landranger 69; OS Explorer 361	94
7	Lochranza	Blackwaterfoot	17 miles (27km)	7 hours	OS Landranger 69; OS Explorer 361	107
8	Blackwaterfoot	Kildonan	12 miles (19km)	6 hours	OS Landranger 69; OS Explorer 361	118
9	Kildonan	Brodick	15 miles (24km)	7 hours	OS Landranger 69; OS Explorer 361	130
10	Ardrossan	Largs	15 miles (24km)	5 hours	OS Landranger 70 and 63; OS Explorer 341	145
11	Largs	Skelmorlie	9 miles (14.5km) by High Road; 7 miles (11km) by Low Road	3 hours via Low Road; 4 hours via High Road	OS Landranger 63; OS Explorer 341	157

APPENDIX B

Accommodation

Ayrshire

The Ayrshire coast can be extremely busy, particularly during the summer, so it is advisable to book accommodation well in advance. The following is a list of recommended options.

Ballantrae

- Kings Arms Hotel 01465 831202
  info@kingsarmsballantrae.com
  www.kingsarmsballantrae.com

- Lagganholm Cottage 01465 831504

- Thistles Cottage B&B 01465 831200
  www.thistlescottage.com

- The Haven 01465 831306

Lendalfoot

- Bennane Shore Holiday Park
  01465 891233
  info@bennaneshore.com
  www.bennaneshore.com

Girvan

- Woodland Bay Hotel 01465 710700
  stay@woodlandfarm.co.uk
  www.woodlandbayhotel.co.uk

- The Royal Hotel 01465 714203
  info@royalhotelgirvan.com
  www.royalhotelgirvan.com

- The Southfield Hotel 01465 714222
  info@thesouthfieldhotel.co.uk
  www.thesouthfieldhotel.co.uk

- Corra Linn B&B 01465 712178
  www.corralinn.co.uk

- Strathavon Caravan Park 01465 712262

Turnberry

- Turnberry Resort 01655 331000
  turnberry@luxurycollection.com
  www.turnberryresort.co.uk

- Malin Court 01655 331457
  info@malincourt.co.uk
  www.malincourt.co.uk/hotel-welcome

- Fairways B&B 01655 331522
  www.fairways-turnberry.co.uk

Maidens

- Wildings Hotel 01655 331401
  bookings@wildingsrestaurant-hotel.
  co.uk www.wildingshotel.com

- Jameston Farm 01655 331765

Culzean

- Culzean Castle 01655 884455
  culzean@nts.org.uk
  www.culzeanexperience.org

Dunure

- Dunure Inn 01292 500 549

- Fisherton Farm 01292 500223

Alloway

- Brig o' Doon House Hotel
  01292 442466
  brigodoon@costley-hotels.co.uk
  www.brigodoonhouse.com

- Sunnyside B&B 01292 441234
  www.ayrbandb.co.uk

- One Alloway Retreat B&B 01292
  441298 relax@onealloway.co.uk
  www.onealloway.co.uk

Ayr

- Swallow Station Hotel 01292 263268
- Arrandale Hotel 01292 289959
  bookings@arrandalehotel.co.uk
  www.arrandalehotel.co.uk
- Grange View B&B 01292 266680
  info@grange-view.co.uk
  www.grange-view.co.uk
- Coila Guest House 01292 262642
  hazel@coila.co.uk www.coila.co.uk
- Canter Holm B&B 01292 880919
  info@canterholmayr.co.uk
  www.canterholmayr.co.uk

Prestwick

- North Beach Hotel 01292 479069
  info@northbeach.co.uk
  www.northbeach.co.uk
- The Hollies B&B 01292 473514
  www.prestwickaccommodation.com
- Firhill B&B 01292 478225
  info@bedandbreakfastprestwick.co.uk
  www.bedandbreakfastprestwick.co.uk
- Fionn Fraoch B&B 01292 476838
  www.fionnfraoch.com

Troon

- South Beach Hotel 01292 312033
  info@southbeach.co.uk
  www.southbeach.co.uk
- Sandhill House 01292 311801
  reservations@sandhillhouse.com
  www.sandhillhouse.plus.com
- Copper Beech B&B 01292 314100
  http://copperbeech.freeservers.com
- Ardess B&B 01292 311909

Irvine

- Harbourside Hotel 01294 275515
  andy@harbourside.biz
  www.harbourside.biz

- Annfield House Hotel 01294 278903
  info@annfieldhousehotel.co.uk
  www.annfieldhousehotel.com
- Irvine Lodge Guest House
  01294 278181
  www.irvinelodge.co.uk
- Harbour Guest House 01294 276212
  info@irvineguesthouse.co.uk
  www.irvineguesthouse.co.uk
- Braidmead House 01294 274045
  info@braidmead.com
  www.braidmead.com

Stevenston

- Ardeer Steading 01294 465438
  info@ardeersteading.co.uk
  www.ardeersteading.co.uk

Saltcoats

- Laighdykes Guest Cottage
  0871 976 5275
  stay@laighdykes.com
  www.laighdykes.com
- Brooklands B&B 01294 464345

Ardrossan

- The Lauriston Hotel 01294 463771
- Crescent Park House B&B
  01294 464900
  www.crescentparkhouse.co.uk
- Edenmore Guest House 01294 462306
  enquiries@edenmoreguesthouse.co.uk
  www.edenmoreguesthouse.co.uk

Seamill and West Kilbride

- Seamill Hydro 01294 822217
  www.seamillhydro.co.uk
- Carlton Seamill B&B 01294 822075
  carlton@westkilbride.net
  www.carlton-seamill.co.uk
- The Merrick Hotel 01294 822649
  www.merrickhotel.co.uk

Fairlie

- Ferry Row 01475 568687
  info@ferryrow.co.uk
  www.ferryrow.co.uk

Largs

- The Queen's Hotel 01475 675311
  info@queenshotel-largs.co.uk
  www.queenshotel-largs.co.uk

- The Willowbank Hotel 01475 675435
  info@thewillowbankhotel.co.uk
  www.thewillowbankhotel.co.uk

- Tigh-an-Struan Guest House
  01475 670668 info@tighanstruan.com
  www.tighanstruan.com

- St Leonards Guesthouse 01475 673318
  www.stleonardsguesthouse.com

- Tigh-na-Ligh Guest House
  01475 673975 mail@tighnaligh.com
  www.tighnaligh.com

Arran

Arran is very busy throughout the year so it is advisable to book accommodation well in advance. The larger towns have several options but there is also a more limited selection on certain sections. Listings with an asterisk (*) are closed in winter.

Brodick

- Allandale House 01770 302278
  info@allandalehouse.co.uk
  www.allandalehouse.co.uk

- Belvedere Guest House 01770 302397
  belvedere@vision-unlimited.co.uk
  www.visionunlimited.co.uk/belvedere

- Ormidale Hotel 01770 302293
  reception@ormidale-hotel.co.uk
  www.ormidale-hotel.co.uk

- Alltan B&B 01770 302937
  www.alltanarran.co.uk

- Carrick Lodge 01770 302550
  www.carricklodge.co.uk

Corrie

- Corrie Hotel 01770 810273
  info@corriehotel.co.uk
  www.corriehotel.co.uk

Sannox

- Sannox Bay Hotel 01770 810225
  www.sannoxbayhotel.com

- Darven Cottage B&B 01770 810280
  www.darvenarran.co.uk

Lochranza

- Lochranza Hotel 01770 830223
  info@lochranzahotel.co.uk
  www.lochranza.co.uk

- Lochranza Youth Hostel 01770 830631

- Kincardine Lodge 01770 830267
  info@kincardinelodge.co.uk
  www.kincardinelodge.co.uk

- CastleKirk B&B 01770 830202
  info@castlekirkarran.co.uk
  www.castlekirkarran.co.uk

Catacol

- Catacol Bay Hotel 01770 830231
  www.catacol.co.uk

Pirnmill

- * Clisham B&B 01770 850294
  clisham@arrannames.co.uk
  www.arran-clisham.co.uk

Machrie

- Achabhealaidh B&B 01770 840360
  www.machriebandb.co.uk

Blackwaterfoot

- Kinloch Hotel 01770 860444
  reservations@kinlochhotel.eclipse.co.uk
  www.bw-kinlochhotel.co.uk

- * Blackwaterfoot Lodge 01770 860202
  info@blackwaterfoot-lodge.co.uk
  www.blackwaterfoot-lodge.co.uk
- Laighbent B&B 01770 860405
  www.laighbent.co.uk
- The Greannan B&B 01770 860200
  www.thegreannan.co.uk

Kilmory

- The Lagg Hotel 01770 870255
  info@lagghotel.com
  www.lagghotel.com

Kildonan

- Kildonan Hotel 01770 820207
  info@kildonanhotel.com
  www.kildonanhotel.com
- Seal Shore Camping & Touring Site
  01770 820320
  enquiries@campingarran.com
  www.campingarran.com
- * Mare B&B 01770 820375
  info@mare-arran.co.uk

Whiting Bay

- * Burlington Hotel 01770 700255
  www.burlingtonarran.co.uk
- Royal Arran Hotel 01770 700286
  www.royalarran.co.uk
- Viewbank Guest House 01770 700326
  www.viewbank-arran.co.uk
- Ellangowan B&B 01770 700784
  ellangowan@arranwelcome.co.uk
  www.arranwelcome.co.uk/ellangowan
- Mingulay 01770 700346
  mingulay@arranwelcome.co.uk
  www.arranwelcome.co.uk/mingulay

Lamlash

- Glenisle Hotel 01770 600559
  enquiries@glenislehotel.com
  www.glenislehotel.com
- Lamlash Bay Hotel 01770 600844
  www.lamlashbayhotel.co.uk
- Lilybank Guesthouse 01770 600230
  www.lilybank-arran.co.uk
- Altachorvie B&B 01770 600468

Attractive cottages line the shore at Corrie

APPENDIX C
Public transport options

Mainland

Ballantrae – Glenapp

Stagecoach West Scotland 358 bus runs between Main Street, Ballantrae and Glenapp Church

Girvan – Ballantrae

Stagecoach West Scotland 358 bus runs between Knockcushan Street, Girvan and Main Street, Ballantrae

Dunure – Girvan

Option 1: Ayrways Coaches 361 bus runs between Castle Road, Dunure and Carrick Road, Ayr; Stagecoach West Scotland 58 bus runs between Carrick Road, Ayr and Knockcushan Street, Girvan

Option 2: Ayrways Coaches 361 bus runs between Castle Road, Dunure and Miller Road, Ayr; Scotrail Glasgow Central to Stranraer train runs between Ayr and Girvan

Troon – Dunure

Scotrail Glasgow Central to Ayr train runs between Troon and Ayr; Ayrways Coaches 361 bus runs between Smith Street, Ayr and Castle Road, Dunure

Ardrossan – Troon

Scotrail Ardrossan Harbour to Glasgow Central train runs between Ardrossan Town and Kilwinning; Scotrail Glasgow Central to Ayr train runs between Kilwinning and Troon

Largs – Ardrossan

Option 1: Stagecoach West Scotland 585 bus runs between Main Street, Largs and Princes Street, Ardrossan

Option 2: Scotrail Largs to Glasgow Central train runs between Largs and Ardrossan South Beach

Skelmorlie – Largs

McGill's Buses 901 bus runs between Shore Road, Skelmorlie and Main Street, Largs.

Arran

Lochranza – Brodick

Stagecoach West Scotland 324 bus runs between Lochranza Pier and Brodick Ferry Terminal. The Caledonian MacBrayne ferry between Brodick and Ardrossan takes you back to the mainland.

Blackwaterfoot – Lochranza

Stagecoach West Scotland 324 bus runs between Blackwaterfoot harbour and Lochranza. The Lochranza to Claonaig ferry can be caught here. If catching the Brodick to Ardrossan ferry, the bus continues to Brodick Ferry Terminal. Another option to catch the ferry is to take the Stagecoach West Scotland 322 bus that runs between Blackwaterfoot harbour and Brodick Ferry Terminal

Kildonan – Blackwaterfoot

Stagecoach West Scotland 323 bus runs between Kildonan Hotel and Blackwaterfoot harbour. If catching the Brodick to Ardrossan ferry, take the Stagecoach West Scotland 323 bus that runs between Kildonan Hotel and Brodick Ferry Terminal

Please check before walking the routes as public transport information is liable to change. See Appendix D for contact details.

APPENDIX D
Useful information

Public transport

Glasgow Prestwick Airport 0871 223 0700
(UK), 00 44 1292 511000 (International)
www.gpia.co.uk

P&O Ferries 0871 66 44 999
(UK) 01 407 34 34 (ROI)
www.poferries.com

Caledonian MacBrayne 01475 650100
www.calmac.co.uk

Scotrail 0845 601 5929
www.scotrail.co.uk

Scottish Citylink 0871 266 33 33
www.citylink.co.uk

Stagecoach 01292 613 500
www.stagecoachbus.com

McGill's Buses 08000 51 56 51
www.mcgillsbuses.co.uk

Ayrways Coaches 01292 738118

Tourist information centres

Girvan

Bridge Street, Girvan KA26 9HH
01465 715500

Ayr

22 Sandgate, Ayr KA7 1BW
01292 290300

Largs

Railway Station, Main Street,
Largs KA30 8AN
01475 689962

Brodick

The Pier, Isle of Arran,
Brodick KA27 8AU
01770 303776

Places of interest

Culzean Castle
www.culzeanexperience.org

Robert Burns Birthplace Museum
www.burnsmuseum.org.uk

Scottish Maritime Museum
www.scottishmaritimemuseum.org

Brodick Castle
www.nts.org.uk/Property/13

Portencross Castle
www.portencrosscastle.org.uk

Kelburn Castle
www.kelburnestate.com

Largs Viking Festival
www.largsvikingfestival.com

Vikingar!
http://www.largsonline.co.uk/vikingar.html

Online information

The Ayrshire and Arran Tourist Board
www.ayrshire-arran.com

The Scottish Outdoor Access Code
www.outdooraccess-scotland.com

The Community of Arran Seabed Trust
(COAST) www.arrancoast.com

Tide times
www.bbc.co.uk/weather/coast/tides

CICERONE GUIDES TO THE BRITISH ISLES

BRITISH ISLES CHALLENGES, COLLECTIONS AND ACTIVITIES

The End to End Trail
The Mountains of England and Wales
   1 Wales & 2 England
The National Trails
The Relative Hills of Britain
The Ridges of England, Wales and Ireland
The UK Trailwalker's Handbook
Three Peaks, Ten Tors

MOUNTAIN LITERATURE

Unjustifiable Risk?

UK CYCLING

Border Country Cycle Routes
Cycling in the Peak District
Lands End to John O'Groats Cycle Guide
Mountain Biking in the Lake District
Mountain Biking on the South Downs
The Lancashire Cycleway

SCOTLAND

Backpacker's Britain
   Central and Southern Scottish Highlands
   Northern Scotland
Ben Nevis and Glen Coe
North to the Cape
Not the West Highland Way
Scotland's Best Small Mountains
Scotland's Far West
Scotland's Mountain Ridges
Scrambles in Lochaber
The Ayrshire and Arran Coastal Paths
The Border Country
The Central Highlands

The Great Glen Way
The Isle of Mull
The Isle of Skye
The Pentland Hills: A Walker's Guide
The Southern Upland Way
The Speyside Way
The West Highland Way
Walking in Scotland's Far North
Walking in the Cairngorms
Walking in the Hebrides
Walking in the Ochils, Campsie Fells and Lomond Hills
Walking in Torridon
Walking Loch Lomond and the Trossachs
Walking on Harris and Lewis
Walking on Jura, Islay and Colonsay
Walking on the Isle of Arran
Walking on the Orkney and Shetland Isles
Walking the Galloway Hills
Walking the Lowther Hills
Walking the Munros
   1 Southern, Central and Western Highlands
   2 Northern Highlands and the Cairngorms
Winter Climbs Ben Nevis and Glen Coe
Winter Climbs in the Cairngorms
World Mountain Ranges: Scotland

NORTHERN ENGLAND TRAILS

A Northern Coast to Coast Walk
Backpacker's Britain Northern England
Hadrian's Wall Path
The Dales Way

The Pennine Way
The Spirit of Hadrian's Wall

NORTH EAST ENGLAND, YORKSHIRE DALES AND PENNINES

Historic Walks in North Yorkshire
South Pennine Walks
The Cleveland Way and the Yorkshire Wolds Way
The North York Moors
The Reivers Way
The Teesdale Way
The Yorkshire Dales Angler's Guide
The Yorkshire Dales
   North and East
   South and West
Walking in County Durham
Walking in Northumberland
Walking in the North Pennines
Walking in the Wolds
Walks in Dales Country
Walks in the Yorkshire Dales
Walks on the North York Moors – Books 1 & 2

NORTH WEST ENGLAND AND THE ISLE OF MAN

A Walker's Guide to the Lancaster Canal
Historic Walks in Cheshire
Isle of Man Coastal Path
The Isle of Man
The Ribble Way
Walking in Cumbria's Eden Valley
Walking in Lancashire
Walking in the Forest of Bowland and Pendle
Walking on the West Pennine Moors
Walks in Lancashire Witch Country

Walks in Ribble Country
Walks in Silverdale
  and Arnside
Walks in the Forest
  of Bowland

LAKE DISTRICT
Coniston Copper Mines
Great Mountain Days in
  the Lake District
Lake District Winter Climbs
Lakeland Fellranger
  The Central Fells
  The Mid-Western Fells
  The Near Eastern Fells
  The North-Western Wells
  The Southern Fells
  The Western Fells
Roads and Tracks of
  the Lake District
Rocky Rambler's Wild Walks
Scrambles in the Lake District
  North & South
Short Walks in Lakeland
  1 South Lakeland
  2 North Lakeland
  3 West Lakeland
The Cumbria Coastal Way
The Cumbria Way and the
  Allerdale Ramble
The Lake District
  Anglers' Guide
Tour of the Lake District

**DERBYSHIRE, PEAK DISTRICT
AND MIDLANDS**
High Peak Walks
The Star Family Walks
Walking in Derbyshire
White Peak Walks
  The Northern Dales
  The Southern Dales

SOUTHERN ENGLAND
A Walker's Guide to the
  Isle of Wight
London – The definitive
  walking guide
The Cotswold Way
The Greater Ridgeway
The Lea Valley Walk
The North Downs Way
The South Downs Way
The South West Coast Path
The Thames Path
Walking in Bedfordshire
Walking in Berkshire
Walking in Kent
Walking in Sussex
Walking in the Isles of Scilly
Walking in the Thames Valley
Walking on Dartmoor
Walking on Guernsey
Walking on Jersey
Walks in the South Downs
  National Park

WALES AND WELSH BORDERS
Backpacker's Britain – Wales
Glyndwr's Way
Great Mountain Days
  in Snowdonia
Hillwalking in Snowdonia
Hillwalking in Wales
  Vols 1 & 2
Offa's Dyke Path
Ridges of Snowdonia
Scrambles in Snowdonia
The Ascent of Snowdon
The Lleyn Peninsula
  Coastal Path
The Pembrokeshire
  Coastal Path
The Shropshire Hills
The Spirit Paths of Wales
The Wye Valley Walk
Walking in Pembrokeshire
Walking on the
  Brecon Beacons
Welsh Winter Climbs

For full information on all our
guides, and to order books and
eBooks, visit our website:
www.cicerone.co.uk.

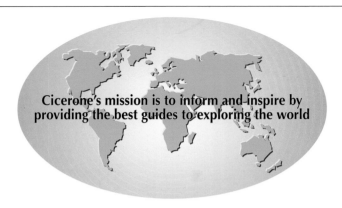

Since its foundation 40 years ago, Cicerone has specialised in publishing guidebooks and has built a reputation for quality and reliability. It now publishes nearly 300 guides to the major destinations for outdoor enthusiasts, including Europe, UK and the rest of the world.

Written by leading and committed specialists, Cicerone guides are recognised as the most authoritative. They are full of information, maps and illustrations so that the user can plan and complete a successful and safe trip or expedition – be it a long face climb, a walk over Lakeland fells, an alpine cycling tour, a Himalayan trek or a ramble in the countryside.

With a thorough introduction to assist planning, clear diagrams, maps and colour photographs to illustrate the terrain and route, and accurate and detailed text, Cicerone guides are designed for ease of use and access to the information.

If the facts on the ground change, or there is any aspect of a guide that you think we can improve, we are always delighted to hear from you.

Cicerone Press
2 Police Square Milnthorpe Cumbria LA7 7PY
Tel: 015395 62069 Fax: 015395 63417
info@cicerone.co.uk www.cicerone.co.uk